AMERICA
IN THE
20TH
CENTURY

1950-1959

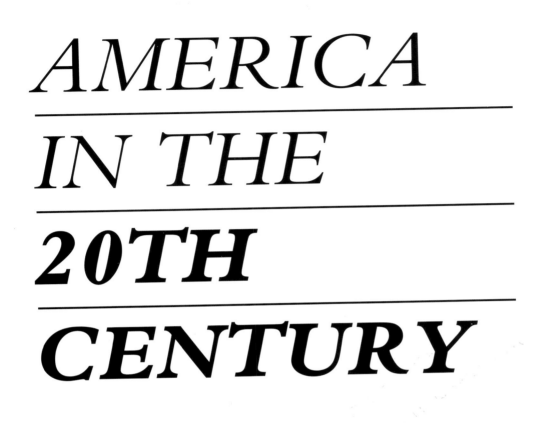

AMERICA IN THE 20TH CENTURY

1950-1959

David Wright and Elly Petra Press

MARSHALL CAVENDISH
NEW YORK • LONDON • TORONTO • SYDNEY

© Marshall Cavendish Corporation 1995

Published by
Marshall Cavendish Corporation
2415 Jerusalem Avenue
PO Box 587
North Bellmore
New York 11710

Library of Congress Cataloging-in-Publication Data
America in the 20th century.
Includes bibliographical references and indexes
Contents: -- [3] 1920-1929/ Janet McDonnell -- [etc.] -- [5] 1940-1949/ Kelli Peduzzi --
[6] 1950-1959/ David Wright and Petra Press -- [etc.]
1. United States -- Civilization -- 20th century.
I. Mc Donnell, Janet, 1962- . II.Wright, David, 1943- . III. Petra Press.
IV. Title: America in the twentieth century.
E169.1.A471872 1995 973.9 94-10854
ISBN 1-85435-736-0 (set)

Series created by The Creative Publishing Company

Series Editor: Paul Humphrey
Academic Consultants: Professor Gregory Bush,
Chair of History Department, University of Miami, Coral Gables
Richard J. Taylor, History Department, University of Wisconsin, Parkside
Marshall Cavendish Editorial Director: Evelyn M. Fazio
Marshall Cavendish Editorial Consultant: Marylee Knowlton
Marshall Cavendish Production Manager: Ruth Toda
Project Editors: Valerie Weber and Helen Dwyer
Picture Research: Gillian Humphrey
Design Concept: Laurie Shock
Designer: Winsome Malcolm

(Frontispiece) *This awesome mushroom cloud signals a tactical nuclear gun being tested at
Frenchman's Flat, Nevada, May 25, 1953.*

Contents

CHAPTER 1
Setting the Stage

Americans: Square on the Surface

The booming decade of the fifties has been called the Nifty Fifties, the Good Old Days, the single decade when hip was hep and good was boss. Looking back, most Americans seemed to be "square," the men carefully dressed in suits and ties, the women with perfect hairdos and perky dresses, more interested in being part of the newly affluent middle class and enjoying their new prosperity than in protesting social inequality or political injustice. The majority of Americans were interested in finding a good, white-collar job with a benevolent company, getting married, having children, and buying a ranch house in the suburbs.

That they were eager to enjoy their new economic freedom is understandable in light of the traumatic events of the previous two decades: a devastating Depression followed by the horrors of World War II. When the young men who fought in Europe and the Pacific for four years returned

The ocean liner Queen Elizabeth, *converted during wartime to a troop ship, is given a warm welcome as it enters New York harbor, full of returning GIs.*

Ira Hayes. (1923-1955)

The only thing sadder than a publicity seeker is maybe a person who shuns publicity but is forced unwittingly into the limelight. Ira Hayes was such a person, and it cost him his life. . . .

Hayes was an American Indian, a member of the Pima tribe, born in the tiny town of Sacaton, Arizona. The eldest of four boys, he was the quiet son of a farm couple. The family was poor, living for a while in a one-room adobe hut with a dirt floor. They were patriotic and religious; one wall of the home was covered with the American flag, and another displayed biblical symbols and pictures.

Ira stood five feet, seven inches and weighed 136 pounds on December 7, 1941, the day the Japanese bombed Pearl Harbor. World War II began for the United States with a declaration of war the following day. Pimas had a history of soldiering, from fighting the Apaches in Arizona to combat against the Germans in France in World War I. Hayes proudly enlisted in the U.S. Marine Corps in the summer of 1942.

Hayes and his family knew about prejudice from white residents of Arizona. The young recruit suffered silently when fellow marines kidded him about carrying a tomahawk or called him "heap big chief." Once the soldiers got to know Hayes, however, the taunting stopped and a deep friendship began. Thrown together in a California boot camp, men from many different ethnic groups learned they had much in common. When friends of Hayes called him chief, he broke into a smile.

The marines had the unenviable task of leading U.S. forces across the Pacific, retaking islands from the Japanese in vicious fighting amid terrible heat and driving rain. The Japanese were trained never to surrender, and this cost the lives of several of Ira's friends. Overrun Japanese soldiers frequently blew up themselves and the marines rather than allowing their capture. Hayes wasn't talkative, but such events made a lasting impression.

Hayes carried a Browning Automatic Rifle and somehow managed to stay in one piece all the way to a Japanese home island, Iwo Jima. There, in February, 1945, the marines ran into enemy forces hidden in tunnels and suffered incredible casualties. After days of unending battle, Hayes and five other marines raised the U.S. flag atop Mount Surabachi, the island's only hill.

For better or worse, a wire service photographer was there to record the scene. Just three of the six men would survive the war, but those in the photo became instant heroes nationwide. Two of the dead men in the photo were misidentified, and this bothered Hayes. But the marines told him to keep quiet about the mistake, and the hypocrisy of this decision

Ira Hayes (right) with fellow heroes of Iwo Jima John H. Bradley and Rene Gagnon.

gnawed at him. He became a civilian and bounced around a number of jobs, drinking heavily. Not even a campaign to rehabilitate him by the wife of pop singer Dean Martin had a lasting effect. Hayes showed up puffy and aged in Washington in 1954 to dedicate the Iwo Jima memorial to the nation's marines. He was only thirty-one.

He returned to Arizona, but the best job he could find was picking cotton. On a cold January night in 1955, Hayes drank himself to sleep in an abandoned adobe hut and froze to death. He was buried with full military honors in Arlington National Cemetery, a delayed casualty of war.

Fifties cars were smarter, faster, and sleeker than their predecessors — the perfect accessory to park outside your new ranch house. Who could resist this 1951 Ford Custom Fordor sedan with its "Fordomatic" Drive transmission, dual spinner radiator grille, and long wraparound chrome fenders?

home to their sweethearts, they wanted to get on with their lives and forget about the death and destruction overseas. It only makes sense that the focus was on fun and innocence, on "I Love Lucy," rock 'n' roll, backyard barbecues, and being part of the status quo.

But the fifties were *not* just a time of fun and innocence, of Buddy Holly, hula hoops, 3-D movies, hot rods, Mickey Mantle, and "Howdy Doody." As much as they wanted to, Americans could not turn their backs on the rest of the world and concentrate on their own prosperity. They emerged from World War II believing fervently in the system of capitalism and feeling that the U.S. had a moral destiny to make the world safe for democracy. The death and destruction of the world war ended in 1945, but they were followed by a decade of a tense and frightening Cold War and a nuclear arms race that made most Americans feel anxious and cautious. They were also haunted daily by the terrors of witch hunts for potential Communists, and deadly atomic tests. The safe thing to do was to conform as much as possible. Religion, home life, respectability, security, compliance with the system — these became the important values.

A booming postwar economy gave middle-class Americans more money than they ever had before. Suburbia, fast cars, and new highways provided an escape from the decaying inner cities and became the central features of the new American scene. Thousands of tracts of land were bulldozed to build housing developments of tiny ranch houses surrounded by shopping centers, schools, churches,

and parking lots. Between 1950 and 1960, the number of American homeowners increased by over nine million, and the number of cars increased by over twenty-one million; over forty thousand miles of interstate highways were built to accommodate these new suburban developments.

Americans not only had more money in the postwar economic boom, they also had more leisure time. While Americans before the war had struggled just to survive the Depression, Americans in 1950 had more time and money to travel, garden, drink, watch TV, read, hunt, listen to music, even paint by numbers, than ever before. It became very fashionable to "do it yourself," which included everything from hanging your own wallpaper to building your own sailboat. Americans prided themselves on the fact that they could do just about anything themselves.

Social Inequities Below the Surface

But the fifties were far more complex than they seemed on the surface. While the middle class was blooming, the nation's poor were getting poorer and urban slums were deteriorating.

Wives of World War II veterans choose the location for their new house in Levittown, the first of William Levitt's mass-constructed housing developments. Showing them the new houses is William Levitt himself. Thousands of acres of agricultural land were to disappear under concrete in order to create a new suburban society and dream homes for returning GIs and their families.

"What was good for our country was good for General Motors and vice versa."

Charles Wilson, secretary of defense, 1953

When millions of World War II soldiers went to Europe and Asia to fight the war, women and minority groups had taken over many of the industrial and service jobs formerly reserved for white males only. While this did much to improve their standard of living during the war years, the return of U.S. soldiers after the war also meant a return in many respects to the old reality. This was especially true for women, whose rightful place, in the fifties at least, was back in the family kitchen. While the average annual income for middle-class whites increased quite dramatically through the decade, the average annual income for African-Americans and other minorities actually decreased.

Although the fifties was a decade of racial integration into all areas of American life, it was a hard-fought battle and racial tensions escalated throughout the decade. Minorities were still being denied the educational and job opportunities that would have helped them achieve economic equality. Women, whatever their color, were still considered inferior and faced discrimination and exploitation both at home and at work. Protest against these social inequalities was beginning to ferment under the bland surface of everyday fifties life.

Some people fondly remember the ideal American family, the golden age of television, and a national return to spirituality during the fifties. In reality, these were just myths the media promoted to disguise what was happening beneath the surface: the conspicuous consumerism, the exploitation of women and minorities, and a dangerous, imperialistic nationalism. By the end of the decade, many Americans, especially young people, felt lost and confused. Stu-

dents became politically active, as more and more citizens lost their unwavering faith in the moral superiority of the United States. Racial tensions, increasing poverty, and political unrest all helped set the stage for the dramatic changes the sixties would bring.

The U.S. as a Prosperous World Superpower

What brought about these dramatic changes? The most important influence was America's involvement in World War II. Although the war had already been over for five years before the fifties started, it continued to have a strong impact on U.S. policy, both at home and throughout the world. World War II had profoundly changed the old world order and the role the U.S. played in it. The alliance of Great Britain, the USSR, and the United States had defeated the Fascist governments of Germany, Italy, and Japan (the Axis alliance), but at a terrible price. Besides killing millions of soldiers and civilians, the war physically crippled what had once been the dominating powers of Europe. The United States, however, was saved from this destruction because the battles were fought on foreign soil, added to which it was the only country to have the atom bomb. America emerged from the war easily the strongest and most prosperous economic power in the world.

The only other country to benefit from the outcome of the war was the Soviet Union. Although it suffered horrible losses in both life and property, the USSR had recruited the largest land army in the history of the world. After the war, Soviet dictator Josef

Stalin used this army to bring eastern Europe, North Korea, and other areas under Soviet control.

By the end of World War II, the United States and the Soviet Union had become the two world superpowers. Although they were bitter enemies by the 1950s, in the summer of 1945 the two countries celebrated (along with the British) their joint victory over the Axis powers. There was much hope throughout the world that, with the help of the newly created United Nations, the U.S. and the Soviet Union would lead the world into a permanent period of international cooperation and world peace.

That hope did not last long. Stalin considered capitalism to be the main enemy of communism and loudly warned western democracies that he had every intention of fighting that enemy. At the same time, he set up satellite Communist states in eastern Europe and Asia and set his sights on the emerging countries of the developing world.

President Truman quickly sent U.S. military and economic aid to help rebuild western European countries and provided military assistance to countries such as Greece, which were being threatened by a Communist takeover. That threat became even more frightening to Americans when, in 1949, Russia successfully tested its own version of the atom bomb. This not only ended the American monopoly, it started a whole new age of warfare and a fearful era that would come to be known as the Cold War.

Cold War is the term given to the ideological and economic competition waged between the United States and the Soviet Union for world dominance. It was a war waged in the decades following World War II by any means short of direct military confrontation — but always in the shadow of the threat of that confrontation. After the war, each power amassed a stockpile of nuclear weapons that could (and probably would) have annihilated the other if such a confrontation had ever taken place. Instead, indirect confrontations occurred as the superpowers competed for world markets and political influence. Thus the ideological system of capitalistic democracy was pitted against that of communism.

When Soviet dictator Josef Stalin clamped control over eastern Europe between 1945 and 1947 by effectively taking over the governments of

Soviet dictator Josef Stalin was dedicated to strengthening the USSR's position as world superpower by spreading communism further through eastern Europe and Asia. His frank commitment to the destruction of capitalism resulted in a struggle for world supremacy between the Soviet Union and the United States, which, constantly poised on the edge of a nuclear confrontation, was to threaten the cozy lives of middle-class Americans throughout the decade.

Harry S Truman, thirty-third president of the United States, was staunchly anticommunist. The sign on his desk said: "The buck stops here," but the continuing Cold War between the U.S. and USSR took its toll and Truman decided not to run again for the presidency in 1952.

Poland, Czechoslovakia, and East Germany, western powers accused him of cordoning off a new Russian empire with an "iron curtain." In response, the U.S. and western European powers (led by President Truman) formed NATO, the North Atlantic Treaty Organization, to counter this new threat. The U.S. also instituted the Marshall Plan, which pumped $17 billion into the rebuilding of war-torn western European countries — and into maintaining a military occupation of those countries.

But in spite of Truman's efforts to contain it, communism continued to spread throughout eastern Europe and developing nations. As communism spread, so did the Cold War, as the U.S. used the Central Intelligence Agency (CIA) to overthrow any developing nation's government suspected of turning procommunist. The nuclear arms race escalated, and one crisis after another flared up throughout the fifties and sixties in Africa, the Far East, Europe, and Central and South America.

The Red Scare

Paranoia in the fifties over the spread of communism (sometimes called the Red Scare) actually began in the twenties and early thirties. Part of the cause was Americans' ignorance of the ideologies of communism, socialism, and even capitalism, or what they really meant. Many thought communism and socialism were the same thing. Some even thought that Franklin D. Roosevelt's New Deal in the thirties intended to help end the Depression was part of a Communist plot to overthrow the United States.

Many people failed to realize that under capitalism (or private enterprise) in its purest form, businesses, industry, and farms are owned by private individuals with no government regulation or interference. *True* capitalism does not exist in the U.S. or anywhere else in the world. Private enterprise needs some form of government regulation to prevent monopolies and to protect the rights of workers and consumers. Most people still mistakenly believe that the U.S. and other western capitalist countries operate under a "pure" form of capitalism in which government noninterference is guaranteed by the Constitution.

Like capitalism, socialism is another economic ideology that developed during the industrial revolution of the eighteenth and nineteenth centuries. Unlike capitalism, however, socialism holds that all businesses, industry, and farms should be owned collectively by the people. Socialists believe that equality, social justice, and individual freedom can only be achieved through the elimination of capitalism.

In the mid-nineteenth century, two Germans named Karl Marx and Frederick Engels took the concept of socialism one step further and developed Marxist communism. They believed that capitalism exploited workers throughout the world and that these workers were becoming increasingly angry and would eventually overthrow capitalism. In its place, these revolutionaries would set up what Marx called a "dictatorship of the proletariat," a system in which private ownership was abolished and all businesses were publicly owned. This temporary form of socialism would then gradually be phased out to make way for true communism.

Under true communism, there would no longer be any need for government, social classes, laws, or politics because greed would be eliminated. Everyone would gladly work to the best of their ability and be given only those goods they needed to survive. Like pure capitalism, true communism does not exist anywhere in the world either. Many Americans in the fifties confused socialism and communism, unfairly branding the country's pro-American Socialist party as "commie pinkos."

The Soviet Empire

Ignorance of ideological differences was not the only reason Americans were getting paranoid about the spread of communism. Another reason was the stereotypical view many Americans had of the Russian Communists. They saw them as evil, barbaric, vodka-guzzling atheists who were plotting to brutally overthrow the U.S. government and brainwash American children.

The fear of communism became so great that in 1938 Congress established the House Un-American Activities Committee (HUAC) to investigate potential Communist subversives living in the United States. After the end of World War II, when the Soviet Union developed its own atom bomb and the Cold War became more threatening, federal, state, and local governments all across the country started their own campaigns to expose and deport the Communists they were sure were to be found lurking in the government, schools, newspaper staffs, church groups, labor unions, and even in the movie industry.

Another reason for the increasing atmosphere of fear and suspicion was the widespread (and incorrect) belief that Russia was too backward a nation to ever have developed the atom bomb by itself; they must have gotten the secret from spies and traitors. But perhaps the biggest reason for the Red Scare was the rapid spread of communism throughout eastern Europe and the Far East.

Communism Spreads to China

Nothing stunned the American public more than the Communist overthrow of China. For years, the U.S. had been supporting Chinese leader Chiang Kai-shek in his civil war against the Chinese Communist forces of Mao Zedong. But instead of spending the money on weapons and training for his troops, and improving conditions for the millions of starving Chinese peasants, Chiang Kai-shek and his equally corrupt top government officials used the money for themselves.

Mao's well-trained Communist army found it easy to outsmart Chiang's poorly trained, badly equipped forces, and in 1948 and 1949 began winning more and more battles. Mao's success was also thanks to his repeated promises to the Chinese peasants of a better life under communism. He finally captured the capital city of Peking (now Beijing) in January of 1949 and forced Chiang to flee to the small island of Formosa (Taiwan) where he was protected by the American fleet.

Americans were shocked and outraged when China fell to the Communists. Most Americans knew very little about Chinese history or about Chiang's corrupt government. Instead of believing that China had been lost because of Chiang's greed and incompetence, they chose to believe it was because the Truman administration was soft on communism and hadn't given Chiang's nationalists enough support.

Americans realized that the spread of communism was throwing the world into a new era of crises. The devastation and horrors of World War II did not bring the world peace so many Americans had hoped for.

World War II Helps the Economy Prosper

The war, however, did bring an end to the terrible Depression of the thirties and early forties. The U.S. had spent over $360 billion on military needs to fight the war, and the spending also created a tremendous boom in industrial production and overall economic prosperity. When sixteen million men and women joined the U.S. Army, Navy and Marine Corps, thousands of job opportunities opened up for women and minority groups they never would have been eligible for otherwise, and those jobs meant money to spend.

At the same time, the demand for high-tech weapons supported hundreds of new businesses. After the war, the sophisticated developments in military defense technology (jet aircraft, rockets, computers, and the creation of synthetic materials such as nylon and plastic) were applied to advancements in consumer products and space exploration.

Although defense spending was no longer allocated to waging war, American politicians felt the need to stay ahead in the arms race to support the Cold War. Thus, the spread of communism helped the economic good times continue, bolstered by the large defense budget. Consumer spending was also booming. The GI Bill of Rights gave returning soldiers opportunities for higher education and low-cost home loans, which offered many people the opportunity to substantially improve their standard

Mao Zedong's Communist army easily overran the corrupt U.S.-backed regime of Chiang Kai-shek in China in 1949, putting nearly one quarter of the world's population — close on 500 million people — under Communist rule. Criticism was levelled at America's Democratic administration, which refused to step in and help Chiang Kai-shek's crumbling nationalist government. In fact, previous U.S. military aid to the country had been filtered into the private purses of Chinese government officials instead of being used for defense.

of living. By 1950, not only were people making more money, they were able to spend that money on new homes, fast cars, and modern household appliances.

As a result, most Americans entered the fifties both excited and worried. The threats of potential nuclear annihilation and Communist takeover were frightening, yet at the same time it was exhilarating to realize that they lived in the richest and most powerful nation in the world.

It was still a white man's nation, however, in which women, African-

Americans, and other minorities were treated as second-class citizens. While the fifties would bring even more technological and economic growth, it would also bring more social conflict as these minorities began demanding equal rights and an end to discrimination. Being a superpower would also bring the U.S. heavy responsibilities in conflicts all over the world, especially in Korea. The fifties are often thought of as a time when things were laid back and nothing really changed. In reality, exactly the opposite was true.

CHAPTER 2
The Joys of Capitalism

Late fifties automobiles were big and brash, like this 1957 Lincoln, with huge tail-fins, whitewall tires, and chrome fenders the order of the day. By the end of the decade, private cars would be the primary means of transport and owners liked their cars to be comfortable as well as a suitably ostentatious status symbol.

Several events took place in the 1950s that would change forever the look and feel of the United States. Among the most important was passage of the federal Interstate Highway Act of 1956. This landmark bill provided for the construction of forty-one thousand miles of freeways, to be built over a ten-year period at a cost of $26 billion. The act represented one of the largest public-works projects

ever undertaken in the United States. As it turned out, interstate highway construction lasted more than twenty-five years and cost more than $100 billion. But the web of wonderful, multilane roads from one major city to another became a necessity, due in part to the huge numbers of cars that were being sold.

Memories of the decade are filled with large, shiny, tail-finned automobiles. That's because Detroit was building barge-sized cars, and Americans were buying them in record numbers. Miles traveled by automobile in 1950 totaled 458 billion. A decade later, that number had doubled. Americans were moving around almost exclusively in private transportation in cars featuring huge V-8 engines, padded dashboards, wraparound windshields, vast expanses of chrome and sheet metal, and even, in some cases, air conditioning. Almost 58 million cars were manufactured during the 1950s, and the 7.9 million vehicles sold in 1955 would not be exceeded until well into the following decade.

If highways and cars were changing the country, so was the housing market. The Great Depression of the 1930s and World War II combined to stifle home construction. So when GIs returned to the U.S. in the mid-1940s, the demand for decent places to live was incredible. That demand was answered by people like William J. Levitt, the first person to offer inexpensive, assembly-line housing. Levitt's Levittowns — hundreds of

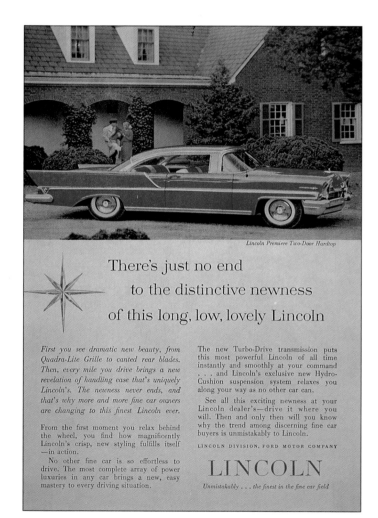

Lincoln Premiere Two-Door Hardtop

There's just no end
to the distinctive newness
of this long, low, lovely Lincoln

First you see dramatic new beauty, from Quadra-Lite Grille to canted rear blades. Then, every mile you drive brings a new revelation of handling ease that's uniquely Lincoln's. The newness never ends, and that's why more and more fine car owners are changing to this finest Lincoln ever.

From the first moment you relax behind the wheel, you find how magnificently Lincoln's crisp, new styling fulfills itself —in action.

No other fine car is so effortless to drive. The most complete array of power luxuries in any car brings a new, easy mastery to every driving situation.

The new Turbo-Drive transmission puts this most powerful Lincoln of all time instantly and smoothly at your command . . . and Lincoln's exclusive new Hydro-Cushion suspension system relaxes you along your way as no other car can.

See all this exciting newness at your Lincoln dealer's—drive it where you will. Then and only then will you know why the trend among discerning fine car buyers is unmistakably to Lincoln.

LINCOLN DIVISION, FORD MOTOR COMPANY

LINCOLN

Unmistakably . . . the finest in the fine car field

William J. Levitt. (1907-1994)

Life magazine named William J. Levitt one of its one hundred most important Americans of the twentieth century — and no wonder. GIs returning from World War II were met with thousands of new, reasonably priced, well-made Levitt-built homes. The suburbs as we know them today were conceived by Levitt in the late 1940s and the 1950s. He constructed more than seventeen thousand houses at a safe and sanitary distance from factories and inner cities.

Levitt's first mass-produced homes were built on New York's Long Island in an area appropriately named Levittown. The planned development, with small but tidy lots, curbs, gutters, and services, became the prototype for many developments all across the land. It also hastened the country's march from cities to suburbs.

An observer compared Levitt, a Long Island native, to Henry Ford. Neither man invented anything or even improved the technology of the product. What each did instead was bring immense popularity to their respective products and industries. They produced economically priced items in a bigger and bolder way than had been done ever before.

Levitt became world renowned and immensely wealthy. But he failed in later years when he tried to create a Levittown-like area in Florida. At one point, his finances were in such a mess that he was barred from building homes in New York state. He sold his northern development companies to his son in 1968 and later lost millions in a series of failed business ventures both in and out of the country.

In 1990, the New York attorney general accused Levitt of looting the Levitt Foundation, a charity. Levitt agreed to pay $11 million in penalties in 1992, but was able to come up with only $7.7 million. He also was accused of making illegal campaign contributions, though he ended up not paying the $39,000 fine because of age and ill health.

Despite his stormy later dealings, William J. Levitt contributed not only to the lifestyle of the 1950s but also helped increase the number of homeowners and strengthened the middle class.

William Levitt (right), head of Levitt and Sons, inspects copper tubing for the Levittown project.

very similar houses crowded into an instant suburb — sprang up on the East Coast and were soon imitated everywhere. Families could have modern appliances, individual bedrooms, garages, and lawns for as little as $6,000. Veterans could use low-interest loans to aid them in their big purchase, and builders and developers stayed busy for the entire decade, particularly in large areas outside cities where homes by the hundreds were being quickly erected.

These occurrences — highway construction and the overpowering urge to own cars and homes — caused huge social changes. Americans need-ed cars and decent roads to reach sub-urban dwellings and to commute from those dwellings back into the central city, where most of the jobs remained. With such a major, nationwide expan-sion under way, jobs were never more important. The quality and quantity of jobs that paid well were amazing. Unions secured enough money for skilled workers to put them into the middle class, and huge corporations were paying their white-collar accountants, salespeople, and man-agers very well. But in the case of the white-collar employee, money and job security had their price.

Up the Corporate Ladder

Young executives operated under rules that were often unwritten but quite rigid, nevertheless. They were expected to socialize after work as part of their job, to consume liquor with-out visible effect, to dress almost as well as their supervisors, to entertain when required, to join country clubs and at least make the attempt to play golf, and to have a doting and sup-portive family awaiting them when they returned to suburbia each eve-ning. Almost all executives at the time were men. Consequently, wives were forced to operate under different, but equally narrow, guidelines. Women looked after the home and children; they were called "helpmates." They were expected to create a supportive atmosphere that would make the ris-ing-executive husband most produc-tive at work. That meant everything from flawlessly washing and pressing dress shirts to mingling with the other wives at company gatherings.

In return for such obedience to

the corporation, families enjoyed club memberships, baseball games, and picnics; the income from white-collar jobs purchased washers, dryers, freez-ers, bicycles, and new cars and allowed middle-class families to set enough money aside for their children's college education. The official mood was optimism among those who enjoyed conformity. Among single adults, minorities, homosexuals, child-less couples, the elderly, and the poor, the unofficial mood bordered on repression. Yet there were pressures on the middle class, too. The percent-age of working wives increased from 15 percent in 1940 to 30 percent in 1960, but some women who felt forced to stay at home were frustrated that their talents were being wasted.

Tranquilized Living

Many turned to alcohol or, begin-ning in the 1950s, prescription tran-quilizers. Miltown and other tranquilizers were selling at the rate of 1.2 million pounds a year by the end of the decade. Suburban women favored the pills because they were widely prescribed, because unlike alcohol they left no odor, and because they made their boring lives seem more bearable. Contributing to mid-dle-class female woes was media pres-sure to consume. Stay-at-home women were bombarded with radio and television advertising that made anyone not using "new, whiter, brighter" laundry detergents or "cavi-ty fighting" toothpaste feel as if she were shortchanging her family. The five million additional women who went to work during the decade did so to ease the family financial burden but also to escape the mindnumbing rou-

> "The smart woman will keep herself desirable. It is her duty to be feminine and desirable at all times in the eyes of the opposite sex."
>
> Leland Kirdel, *Coronet*, 1953

tine of being stuck at home with little to challenge them intellectually.

Meanwhile, inside the big corporations, men had their own set of pressures. Middle-class people were finding that they frequently had to move from one far-flung location to another in order to climb the corporate ladder. One Connecticut family on the way up moved out of a home not yet sold, into a new home in Illinois, and then back to a different location in Connecticut. Their lightning relocations included buying a new home at each stop, resulting in a brief, stressful period of paying three different mortgages each month! The hardship of multiple moves was offset in part by frequent pay raises, which meant that families could move each time into slightly fancier housing with a few more labor-saving devices.

Madison Avenue Influence

Pressure to buy, buy, buy came from several directions. "Keeping up with the Joneses" meant frequently trading cars, purchasing larger television sets, and being as fashionable as the neighbors. Clues as to what the neighbors would buy next were found on television, on radio, on the explosion of roadside billboards, and in magazines. The advertising business became known as Madison Avenue, due to the number of ad agencies on that street in New York City. Agen-

By the 1950s, a wider choice of processed foods was appearing in the supermarkets. Ready prepared frozen and pre-packed meals meant more leisure time for the family to enjoy, with a whole range of products for between meal snacking.

cies created avalanches of advertising that came at the consumer in subtle and clever ways. Ads accompanying television shows, for examples, were attuned to the audience. "Dragnet," a tough-talking cop show, was sponsored by Chesterfield unfiltered cigarettes favored by men. Comedian Milton Berle, with his general audience, was sponsored by Texaco: Gasoline was needed by all adult drivers. And a flavoring for milk, called Ovaltine, sponsored the popular after-school action adventure, "Captain Midnight."

A Pall Mall ad of 1955. Then smoking was often equated with suave success — in business or in relationships — or with the rugged enjoyment of some outdoor leisure pursuit.

REWARD YOURSELF...

Refresh yourself with "freshly-lit" flavor

In today's high-speed living, the smooth, gentle mildness of a freshly-lit PALL MALL encourages you to ease up . . . put worries aside . . . enjoy life more. Reward yourself with frequent moments of relaxation—get that certain feeling of contentment. Choose well—smoke PALL MALL.

Tastes "freshly-lit" puff after puff

PALL MALL is so fresh and fragrant, so mild and cool and sweet it tastes freshly-lit puff after puff.
Get pleasure-packed PALL MALL in the distinguished red package today.

PALL MALL
FAMOUS CIGARETTES

The Finest Quality Money Can Buy

"WHEREVER PARTICULAR PEOPLE CONGREGATE"

The quality of advertising — scripts, visuals, the ability to reach the intended audience — was wonderful, regardless of whether it was of real benefit. The Marlboro Man, a handsome, leathery cowboy, strongly and silently showed that men smoked and that rugged men smoked Marlboro cigarettes. The cowboy's chiseled features gazed down on commuter traffic from billboards, shone forth at televised football games' half times, and popped up in the center of news magazines. Then there was a funny little imported car called the Volkswagen, designed before World War II as a cheap form of transportation for residents of Hitler's Germany, which used whimsical advertising to reach the two hundred thousand American buyers who, in 1957, were interested in good gas mileage rather than tail-fins and huge, plushy comfort.

The five-day, forty-hour work week became standard, leaving middle-class Americans with time on their hands. Some of this time was taken up in do-it-yourself projects. A great many rolls of wallpaper were hung during the decade by homeowners rather than by professional decorators. Every home sprouted power tools, power lawn mowers, hoses and sprinklers, car waxes and shampoos, rakes, hoes, and shovels.

Much of the equipment seen stacking up in garages or in lawn sheds was purchased on credit as America discovered plastic. Diner's Club was the first to offer a charge-card or credit-card method of payment in 1950. It was joined by American Express, then by cards from major oil companies, then by Sears, Roebuck and Co., and others. Consumer debt more than doubled, from $73 billion to $196 billion, in the decade.

One of the Best Ways
Men get to know Each Other

How well do you know your boy?
Does he really know you? He's growing fast.
Is he growing away from you? Shed those years,
drop that dignity, forget those problems.
Come down out of the clouds and get
down on the floor with your boy and Lionel Trains
this Christmas. It will make him happier and
you a lot younger. Lionel Trains bring a man
and boy closer than anything in the world.
See your dealer for the 1950 catalog or
send coupon for special offer.

start this Christmas
with LIONEL TRAINS

Now with *MAGNE—TRACTION!*
Lionel's track-gripping triumph
that makes trains take amazing grades
and curves. *Plus* realistic built-in whistle,
smoke, remote-control couplers.
And priced lower than
in many years past.

Look at the
JOE DIMAGGIO
LIONEL CLUB HOUSE
TELEVISION SHOW
Every Saturday on NBC Network
See local newspapers
for time and station

LIONEL TRAINS, Post Office Box 392
Madison Square Station, New York 10, N. Y.
I enclose 25c. Please send me special Lionel Train Catalog offer postage
prepaid.
1. The Big New Lionel 44-page full-color catalog
2. The "Magic of Magne-Traction Book" with new track layouts,
scenic effects, landscaping, etc.
3. The Lionel "Portfolio of 19th Century Locomotive Art Prints"—in
color—suitable for framing.

Name
Address
City   Zone   State

Fifties' girls had their Barbie dolls, the boys had their Davy Crockett caps, and model train sets like this one. With their own rooms to play in and more money available to treat the kids, children became targets for advertising as they, too, joined the consumer society.

Mother's Little Helpers

Dad was most often the wielder of the paint brush, the pruning shears, and the insecticide, but Mom had access to a number of handy products too. She heated new and convenient foods labeled "instant" or "frozen," serving them up on the back yard picnic table in good weather or on TV trays when it rained. A middle-class

Fads came and went as new gimmicks were introduced to encourage families to spend more money. Hula hoops had their season. These youngsters are taking part in a polio fundraiser in 1958.

wife ran a roaring vacuum cleaner, she may have had an electric dishwasher and an electric blender, spent as much time defrosting as cooking, and, in the time they saved her, could relax to the bubbling rhythm of an electric coffee percolator. Not all labor-saving devices came in mechanized form — frozen orange juice found its defrosted way onto America's breakfast tables, while the humble potato, disguised in chip form, was consumed in mass quantities. Time seemed important and spare time was what all such purchases gave each household.

After a Saturday of working around the house, the middle class relaxed. They grilled burgers, hot dogs, and steaks outdoors, they drank cocktails, beer, and soft drinks (but not much wine), they watched the children wiggle around the neighborhood inside glowing plastic hula hoops, and they entertained friends and neighbors. They played recordings of Frank Sinatra or Patti Page on their new stereo phonographs, they watched "The Life of Riley" on television, or they crept off to bed with those get-to-the-point inventions, *The Reader's*

Digest Condensed Books. Children listened to rock 'n' roll records on scratchy little portable players, appreciating everyone from Pat Boone and Elvis Presley to Laverne Baker and Screamin' Jay Hawkins. Life, it certainly appeared, was good.

Better Medicine

Life also appeared to last much longer. Synthetic penicillin was developed, which meant that pneumonia and several other diseases were much less capable of killing than before. Drs. Jonas Salk and Albert Sabin, working separately, developed vaccines that helped eliminate polio, a leading crippler of children. Children underwent a number of routine, briefly painful vaccinations and shots, many of them administered by nurses in public school classrooms. Americans took more and more pills and preventives — children in Wisconsin kinder-

Jonas Salk.

Each May and June, kids all over 1950s America headed for their favorite pools, lakes, or swimming holes. Each July and August, those same pools, lakes, or swimming holes would be empty — the public feared polio and kept children away from what they saw as breeding grounds for the child-crippling disease.

All that has changed, thanks to a brilliant scientist and physician named Jonas Salk. Salk earned several degrees, including one in public health, before joining the University of Pittsburgh as a research professor of bacteriology. He served the U.S. Army in World War II by working on a flu vaccine, and he knew more about communicable diseases than anyone.

Infantile paralysis (also called poliomyelitis, or polio) became well known before World War II because President Franklin D. Roosevelt had come down with the disease as a young adult. Thousands of children caught it every summer, often with permanently disabling, or even fatal, results. Salk began to work seriously on the virus after it was isolated by another group of researchers at Harvard in 1949.

By 1952, Salk had created a vaccine made up of a virus he had killed and then injected into healthy people as a preventive. After two years of testing — with a few terrible mistakes — the vaccine was launched on a widespread basis in 1954. Until Albert Sabin introduced an improved vaccine a few years later, the Salk vaccine saved countless children from illness, disfigurement, and death.

The Salk product continued to be used in remote countries, primarily because it did not need refrigeration. Ironically, the Nobel Prize went to John Enders at Harvard, the first scientist to isolate the virus. Salk remained in Pittsburgh until 1963, when he moved to San Diego as founding director of the Salk Institute for Biological Studies.

He married in 1970, only five years before retirement. His wife, Francoise Gilot, was the former girlfriend of another giant of the twentieth century, artist Pablo Picasso.

With instant foods and drinks available, Americans had more time to relax — and to spend some of those spare dollars. This Birds Eye canned orange juice ad is from 1950.

gartens were fed "goiter pills." These were pleasant tasting tablets that were supposed to prevent one kind of vitamin deficiency.

Television prompted the public to take care of itself. Hundreds of now defunct toothpastes such as Ipana, deodorants such as Mum, and tablets such as Carter's Little Liver Pills were dropped into shopping carts alongside conveniences such as TV dinners, instant coffee, and ready-to-eat breakfast cereal. Deodorant could be crucial because very few homes or workplaces were air conditioned. A Chicago *Sun-Times* copy editor began his summer day in a shirt and tie, and, by the afternoon deadline, was seen in an undershirt in the Windy City. Fans moved the air but failed to reduce the temperature. In fact, the first places to be centrally cooled were the better restaurants and movie theaters, which installed air conditioning to lure people away from television sets at home.

Despite the excitement of the movies, families tended to stay at home during the week. There was homework to do, television to watch, pets to play with and care for. Adult males sometimes departed one night a week to bowl in a league or to attend a fraternal group meeting. Fraternal organizations such as the Jaycees, the Lions Club, the Rotary International, the Elks, and the Moose were peopled by the middle class, while the American Legion and Veterans of Foreign Wars appealed to all levels of white society. Females occasionally spent the evening at book clubs or in women's clubs. The latter, like the men's organizations, performed good works such as filling playground boxes with clean sand or planting flowers in public areas.

Middle-Class Values

Suburbanites saw themselves as Republicans, primarily because many of them had grown up admiring Dwight D. Eisenhower, the president from 1952 to 1960. Ike had helped win World War II, was the kind of guy it was hard to stay mad at, had presided over the end of the Korean War, and, except for several recessions, was steering the country on an upward economic spiral. Racist organizations were dormant for the time being, and the most extreme political organization, the ultra-right-wing John Birch Society, did not take shape until 1958. Nevertheless, many of the sons and daughters of those who had backed Franklin D. Roosevelt and the New Deal voted for Ike — and for his vice president, Richard M. Nixon — in 1952 and 1956.

They didn't talk about it much, but members of the middle class had firmly held beliefs. In addition to being active members of a mainline Christian church (Baptist, Methodist, Presbyterian, etc.), they believed themselves to be financially much better off than their parents. They also felt that, given the way the country was expanding, their own children would be even wealthier. Hardly anyone owned stock, and not many had savings accounts worth mentioning. Instead, they put their faith in the corporation, which provided free or low-cost benefits, such as health insurance, retirement plans, and paid vacations. Middle-class white people gave to charities but kept their distance from closer involvement in aiding the poor or the down and out.

For children growing up in the 1950s, life could be more than good. Twelve-year-olds circled the block on pricey, candy-apple colored Schwinn Corvettes or on J. C. Higgins bicycles. From those bikes hung Wilson or MacGregor baseball gloves, Louisville slugger bats, and rugged Lee or Levi denim jackets. The boys wore blue jeans for play and chinos for school or church, while girls put on midcalf-length pedal pushers or shorts for leisure and an array of synthetic wash-and-wear dresses, skirts, and blouses for other occasions. Girls played with dolls, including the ubiquitous Barbie, idolized cowgirl Dale Evans, and checked out the boys on "Dick Clark's American Bandstand." Boys pretended they were Davy Crockett, from the television program, complete with coonskin cap and shirt.

Drive-in movies were a popular way for Americans to spend some of their new leisure time. The drive-in meant you could take in a movie and enjoy a hot dog without leaving the comfort of your plush car. It also gave teenagers a chance to escape the watchful eyes of their parents.

Older kids, especially the boys, didn't mind being thought of as juvenile delinquents. Male teenagers donned engineer's boots, jeans, T-shirts, and leather jackets. They smoked awkwardly, spun the tires on their parents' cars, and leered nervously at girls their age. Young people went out in cars in large numbers, to drive-in or indoor movies, to drive-in restaurants, to school sports events, to dances called sock hops, and to each other's houses for sleepovers and parties. Most boys either wanted to be all-American athletes or bruised loners, while most girls saw themselves ideally as either all-American cheerleaders or young women who didn't mind having less-than-spotless reputations.

The Downside of Progress

Cars, highways, suburbs, and popular culture caused enormous change, not all of it for the better. Though the farm population had been declining

John Kenneth Galbraith.

A generation of American leaders was influenced by Galbraith, a Canadian by birth who taught at Harvard University from 1949 to 1975. Throughout the 1950s, he was probably the only academic economist whose name and face were known to the average American. His tall lanky frame was a familiar sight in Washington, particularly in Democratic administrations in the 1960s.

The nice thing about Galbraith and his work is that he delivers ideas in ways the public can understand. His books are persuasive, funny, and easily absorbed by the general reader. In them, he critiques the twentieth century. Two of his many works came out in the 1950s and enjoyed real popularity. The first, *American Capitalism*, was published in 1952 and explained how the country's capitalistic system worked in a whole new way. It suggested that America's economy was based on two rival, competing forces that varied, depending on the situation.

The second book, *The Affluent Society*, was published in 1958 and compared and contrasted the aggressive spending of huge corporations to the decline in public services and the ongoing problems of the nation's poor. The book influenced the presidencies of John F. Kennedy and Lyndon B. Johnson. In fact, Johnson's War on Poverty economics program lifted ideas from Galbraith's writings.

Galbraith continued to command a wide audience long after the fifties ended. Books such as *The New Industrial State* (1967) and *Economics and the Public Purpose* (1973) were widely read, though some of his fellow economists grew tired of his reliance on planning and management to solve government problems. Yet they honored him in 1972 by electing Galbraith president of the American Economic Association.

An informal advisor to President Kennedy, Galbraith served from 1961 to 1963 as U.S. ambassador to India. His ideas continue to be popular in liberal Democratic and progressive circles.

since 1900, it slid by a sizeable 17 percent during the decade, as an average of 1.4 million persons left rural areas every year for higher-paying city jobs. That reduced the number of people who shopped in isolated small towns, where Friday and Saturday nights had once been lively but which became much less so as the 1950s proceeded. Equally important, the new interstate highways bypassed the modest-sized cities and villages, depriving them of shoppers who had once stopped. Meanwhile, along the new interstate systems, franchises and shopping malls were being constructed. The rural and small-town exodus picked up speed.

But while interstate highways could speed produce to market and goods to outlying areas, they could

The new suburban society of the fifties was perfect for America's family-orientated middle class. Pleasant, if more or less identical, homes in well-planned environments were perfect for the stay-at-home Mom who was the ideal of the decade. But this cozy image did not tell the full story.

also spell trouble. Sociologists soon discovered that the broad ribbons of concrete aided criminals, who now could commit a series of felonies in widely separated locales and be well out of the area. Despite their on- and off-ramps and other safety features, highway deaths nationwide continued to climb. Throughout the fifties, there were five million accidents, forty thousand fatalities, and one hundred thousand people permanently disabled each year. As more and more goods moved by truck, the number of car-truck mishaps increased, usually with grisly results to the drivers of the smaller vehicles. All the while, leaded gasoline pumped pollution from tailpipes into the air that was as potentially deadly as it was invisible.

Television's Mixed Message

Television was everywhere by the end of the decade. It sent odd messages to the poor, many of whom were simply overlooked in the consumer-crazed times. An estimated fifty million people were near or below the poverty line, which hovered around $3,000 for a family of four. Such people were sent frequently unpleasant messages via the mass media. Southerners were portrayed as rustics ("The Real McCoys"), blacks were portrayed as stuttering schemers ("The Amos 'n' Andy Show"), and rural residents were informed subtly and otherwise that the real America began and ended in the suburbs. Meanwhile, for

the poor, convenience foods meant that children might devour such items as Twinkies and bottles of soda as a substitute for breakfast. Yet their plight would not be noticed until the decade that followed — by Democrats like John F. Kennedy and Lyndon B. Johnson, who wanted their votes and gave them federally-funded programs in exchange for political support.

If suburban residents were having large families, so were residents of inner cities. Those who could afford it moved to suburbia, while those who could not moved into neighborhoods that traditionally had been off limits. When a house or apartment building in an ethnic neighborhood (Italian or Polish, for example) was sold or occupied by blacks, the neighborhood frequently changed color within a few months. "For Sale" signs sprouted like weeds, with real estate brokers sometimes using scare tactics to get houses to sell. Realtors and bankers also redlined (refused to sell African-American individuals or other minorities houses or to lend them money for purchases in certain areas), and there were no fair-housing laws on federal, state, or local books. The newly arrived minorities should have been proud of their purchases. Instead, they were made to feel ashamed of their color or language.

Racial Tensions

Race relations deteriorated during the decade, though violent behavior was much more common in the 1960s than in the 1950s. Black-white confrontations, varying in size, duration, and intensity, erupted in Atlanta, Chicago, Cleveland, Indianapolis, Kansas City, Los Angeles, Miami, and

New York City. Because blacks had been moving north since World War I, there were large numbers in northern cities in desperate need of jobs, houses, and schools. They took heart from a U.S. Supreme Court decision in 1954, dubbed *Brown v. the Board of Education of Topeka, Kansas.* The high court decided that "separate-but-equal" schooling was, in fact, not equal. The decision set the stage for the integration of public schools, especially in the South. Central High School in Little Rock, Arkansas, was ringed by federal troops in 1957 to prevent segregationist whites from harming the few African-American students who showed up for classes. Troops separating black and white students became a familiar site on television sets all across the country.

Such scenes only hinted at the bitter confrontations that would become routine in the decade to follow.

Following the U.S. Supreme Court ruling, Brown v. the Board of Education, *in May 1954, that segregation in public schools was unconstitutional, Mrs. Nettie Hunt explains its significance to her daughter Nikie on the steps of the high court building, in Washington, D.C. The Court had concluded that the "separate but equal" policy meant, in effect, "separate facilities [that] are inherently unequal."*

CHAPTER 3
The Ideal Family: Myth and Reality

After the uncertainties of the Depression in the thirties and World War II, young couples at last felt secure enough to marry young and have big families in the fifties. Despite the hard-won fight for emancipation in earlier decades of this century, a woman's place in the fifties was usually in the home. "Ideal" families enjoyed spending time together as a close-knit unit.

When people today long for old-fashioned family values, they may be thinking of childhoods spent in the 1950s. There was a real emphasis on marriage, children, and family life during these ten years. And no wonder. The 1930s had been the decade of the Great Depression, when many families put off having children and lived in crowded shacks, flats, or dilapidated houses often in want of food, heat, or furniture. Much of the 1940s were war years, when women worked and when a father, husband, brother, or boyfriend could march off to battle and possibly return in a wheelchair, or in a box. Americans, by 1950, had had enough deprivation and anguish.

They began to marry at a younger age. In 1900, by way of comparison, men were almost twenty-six and women almost twenty-two when they married. By 1953, nearly one-third of all nineteen-year-old females were married to men who were only about twenty-two. The divorce rate, which had risen slowly since the 1920s to about one marriage in ten, leveled off in the fifties. Divorce was simply socially unacceptable. It reflected badly on white-collar men in particular, who sometimes saw their careers stall because bosses perceived them as irresponsible if they divorced. Women were viewed as victims in a tragedy that was not of their making. One signal that things were changing came in 1960, when America's favorite television couple, Lucille Ball and Desi Arnaz, got a real-life divorce.

Marriages took place in large numbers for many reasons. Though the economy was sometimes shaky, Americans saw the fifties, with its thousands of new products or better designs of old products, as being blessed by progress. Young people could marry with confidence because things were all right now and were

sure to improve further. In fact, the young saw older brothers and sisters living in new houses and driving new cars in suburbia and believed overwhelmingly that this was the good life. Their beliefs were reinforced by TV, where "The Adventures of Ozzie and Harriet," "Leave it to Beaver," and "Father Knows Best" portrayed funny, lovable, and loving families. It was no coincidence that the most combative couple on the tube, Mr. and Mrs. Ralph Cramden (Jackie Gleason and Audrey Meadows in the comedy show, "The Honeymooners") lived in a rundown apartment.

Though kids, by the time they were teenagers, sometimes balked at the notion, families did many things together — they went to church, they went on vacation, they attended family reunions, they saw big-league baseball games, they watched television, they worked in the yard, they washed the car — and they multiplied. Between 1946, when soldiers mustered out of the military, and 1964, when birth control pill use became widespread, men and women made babies. Some thirty million people, most of them children, were added to the census rolls between 1950 and 1960. The birthrate peaked in 1957, with 4.3 million new Americans, and it stayed above four million each year into the 1960s.

There were many reasons for such busy reproduction. One was the Korean War, which encouraged

Family television comedies like "The Honeymooners" were extremely popular during the fifties. Here Ralph (Jackie Gleason), lectures Alice (Audrey Meadows), as Norton (Art Carney) and Trixie (Joyce Randolph) look on.

This is what the typical college student looked like in the 1950s: smart and sensible. The student radicalism that was to become a hallmark of the sixties was still in the distance. For this young student of the University of Vermont, serious study lifted the pressure on her to marry and settle down for a few years.

couples to marry and have at least one child: Single men were inducted into the military before husbands and fathers. But there were many other reasons, including the fact that men and women who did not have children were seen as somehow abnormal. Worse, men were judged by whether they had managed to father at least one son. Dad and Buddy and Sis were often accompanied by Mom, pregnant again, and carrying another young child on her hip. Any stigma over being pregnant evaporated in the 1950s because just about *everybody* seemed to be expecting a baby!

The Role of Women

Women today differ a great deal from the women of the 1950s. However, it would be a mistake to view women of the earlier decade as discontented. At no time during the fifties did a majority of females want their own careers — though there were 19.3 million working women as early as 1951. Many said they were happy to morally support their husband and to serve as a Boy or Girl Scout den mother, be an active member of the local Parent Teacher Association, a Sunday school teacher, or the person on the block who collected for the March of Dimes fund drive to combat polio each year. Few women thought about feminism as it is conceived today. The women's movement earlier in the century was recalled fondly as having won the vote for female adults. At the other extreme, it was blamed for ills such as pacifism, the decline of religious beliefs, and even the Great Depression.

Large numbers of men and women looked on female employment during World War II as strictly an emergency measure. When GIs returned to civilian life, women were laid off so that the ex-soldiers could have jobs. Among those who had developed skills and made serious money, there was bitterness at leaving or sliding down the workforce scale. Overwhelmingly, women were consigned to clerical and other traditional female positions. Women who wanted to make something of themselves tended to go into either teaching or nursing. A few women did attend college to pursue careers in medicine, law, or science. But they were the exception rather than the rule. Those fortunate enough to graduate from better colleges in the East signed on with the editorial departments of magazines or book publishers or went after service work that was similarly fulfilling — though not necessarily financially rewarding.

Almost half of all college students (47 percent) in the 1920s were women. By the 1950s, that number had dropped to 35 percent, in part as a result of the lack of money in the 1930s. Some women's colleges closed and others became coeducational. Perhaps because almost all college instructors were male, college may have seemed less inviting to girls. But after *Sputnik* soared into the heavens, it was pointed out that many Soviet women were doctors and engineers.

At that time, fewer than 20 percent of all science and mathematics majors in American colleges were women. Compared to many other nations at the time, the United States was not using the potential of its female population. But why?

Rigid Gender Roles

Gender roles were narrower and more traditional in American society. Little girls were expected to play with the decade's hottest doll, Barbie, while little boys were steered toward the ultimate warrior, GI Joe. There were no federal regulations concerning equality of opportunity for female athletes, so all public and most private

Riddle: What's college?
That's where girls who are above cooking and sewing go to meet a man they can spend their lives cooking and sewing for.

Ad for Gimbel's campus clothes, 1952

Glamour doll Barbie delighted thousands of little girls and provided the manufacturers with profitable new marketing possibilities by offering an infinite variety of new fashion clothes and accessories for sale. Clearly a girls' toy, Barbie helped define and instill the ideal woman's prime objective into girls at an early age — to look her best to get a man. In 1960, Barbie's friend Ken became a popular doll too.

Semi-formal fashion for men and women in 1954. More disposable income meant both sexes could become interested in the latest look. Permed hair and polka dots were in, as were pinched waists and high heels. Men greased their hair to keep it firmly in place. For the young, however, a more casual look was emerging — jeans, loose sweaters, and tennis shoes.

schools fielded only male teams in sports such as football, basketball, baseball, and track. A few girls played rugged sports like field hockey or half-court basketball, but more often in gym class than anywhere else. Not many teenage girls wanted to be known as tomboys — girls who were as willing as their brothers to climb a tree or kick a football.

Clothing could reflect the primness that was expected of females. Waists were tight, frequently pinched to the point of agony via an undergarment known as the girdle. There were A-line or full skirts, tailored blouses, and tight-fitting sweaters. Parisian designs drifted into the U.S. and were copied as to the height of hemlines

and type of silhouette. Names like Dior, St. Laurent, Givenchy, and Chanel made only occasional sacrifices to comfort, such as the ugly, late-1950s sack dress. Showing off the latest creations were models with large followings. Thin, almost boyish women like Edda Hepburn van Heemstra would become Audrey Hepburn and serve as Hollywood role models in the early part of the next decade. The fifties were a time when the fashions of rich women were copied by everyone else.

Held to impossible standards as they were, women nevertheless excelled where permitted. Writers in particular seemed to come from many walks of life. A Maine housewife

Lena Horne.

Born into a middle-class home in Brooklyn, New York, Lena Horne joined the chorus of Harlem's famed black showplace, the Cotton Club, in 1933 at the age of sixteen. Her beauty quickly attracted attention, and she left to tour nationwide with an orchestra showcasing her pleasing voice. Her first recordings came out in 1939.

She returned to the New York City area during World War II to work at Manhattan's Cafe Society Downtown. Horne went from there to Hollywood, where she became the first black woman to sign a long-term acting contract. This was at a time when most African-American actors and actresses were given only small and unimportant roles as servants, sidekicks, and slaves.

Her films included *Panama Hattie* in 1942, *Cabin in the Sky* and *Stormy Weather* in 1943, and *Meet Me in Las Vegas* in 1956. In 1957, she took a break from her almost nonstop nightclub schedule to star in *Jamaica*, her first Broadway musical. Horne's most popular songs include "Stormy Weather," "Blues in the Night," "The Lady is a Tramp," and "Mad About the Boy."

Described more than once as the most beautiful woman on earth, Horne has a following among intellectuals and jazz fans as well as mainstream Americans. Popular and respected throughout the 1950s, true recognition came a bit later. She won a special Tony Award for her one-woman show, *Lena Horne: The Lady and Her Music,* in 1981.

Other recognitions have followed, including interviews and profiles on network television. Those who always enjoyed her music have only lately become aware that Horne has quietly given time and money over the years to humanitarian causes. She has been among the country's most admired women for more than forty years.

Lena Horne (center) with the Peters Sisters, on their arrival in Paris as part of a 1950 European tour.

named Grace Metalious, scribbling on her kitchen table, penned a novel called *Peyton Place*. It was full of naughty, small-town sex, and it sold six million copies in six months in 1956. In contrast, scientist Rachel Carson was gathering documentation that would soon alert the U.S. and the world to the dangers of pesticides in a book that would be titled *Silent Spring*. Others included journalist Marguerite Higgins, the first woman correspondent to win a Pulitzer Prize; social critics Mary McCarthy and Diane Trilling; black poet Gwendolyn Brooks; and fiction writers Carson McCullers, Flannery O'Connor, and Eudora Welty.

Entertainment has always been a place where the oppressed could express themselves, and numerous women became not just well known in America but enjoyed a following around the world. They were singers Rosemary Clooney, Billie Holiday, Patti Page, Ella Fitzgerald, Lena Horne,

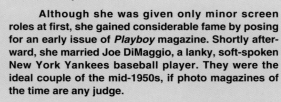

Marilyn Monroe. (1926-1962)

Today's feminists point with justification to the way Marilyn Monroe was manipulated throughout her short life as emblematic of society's desire to keep women in weak, nonthreatening roles. They believe society in general and movie publicity people in particular were the sources of her personal troubles.

Monroe was born Norma Jean Baker, the daughter of a mother prone to fits of depression, in Los Angeles. With her mother frequently confined to an asylum, she spent time in several foster homes before being picked at the age of eighteen to be a model for the armed forces. Her luscious looks gained her a contract with Twentieth Century Fox studios two years later.

Although she was given only minor screen roles at first, she gained considerable fame by posing for an early issue of *Playboy* magazine. Shortly afterward, she married Joe DiMaggio, a lanky, soft-spoken New York Yankees baseball player. They were the ideal couple of the mid-1950s, if photo magazines of the time are any judge.

Monroe suddenly became a major box office attraction, starring in films such as *The Seven-Year Itch* in 1955, *Bus Stop* in 1956, *Some Like it Hot* in 1959, and *The Misfits* in 1961. She was the foremost sex symbol of the postwar years, competing globally with stars such as France's Brigitte Bardot and Italy's Sophia Loren. Her imitators ranged from Jayne Mansfield in the U.S. to Diana Dors in Britain.

She divorced DiMaggio rather quickly and married Arthur Miller, the famed playwright, in 1956. That marriage last five years. Toward the end of her life, still manipulated by studio public relations people, she is said to have had love affairs with President John F. Kennedy and with his younger brother, Bobby, who was then the United States attorney general.

Suffering from the same kind of depression seen in her mother, Monroe ended her life by taking a drug overdose. Her legacy includes tributes to her by writers of stature, including Norman Mailer and Gloria Steinem.

"The more people have studied different methods of bringing up children the more they have come to the conclusion that what good mothers and fathers instinctively feel like doing for their babies is the best after all."

Physician and author
Benjamin Spock

Giselle Mackenzie, Sarah Vaughan, and Pearl Bailey; television comedians Lucille Ball, Imogene Coca, and Eve Arden; and more quality actresses than could be counted. Among these women were Joanne Woodward, Eva Marie Saint, Grace Kelly, Debbie Reynolds, Kim Novak, and Doris Day. Musical comedy talent ranged from Carol Channing to Mary Martin to Gwen Verdon. Actresses exploited strictly for the way they looked included Jayne Mansfield, Jane Russell, and Marilyn Monroe.

Each entertainer possessed qualities that made her quite unique and, therefore, memorable.

Growing Up in the Fifties

A simple, nonfiction book first published in 1947 made a lasting impression on American kids and their parents. The volume was *The Common Sense Book of Baby and Child Care* by Dr. Benjamin Spock. In it, he told parents all the things a mother or grandmother might have told new parents had U.S. society not been so mobile and widespread. Kids raised with Spock were given an informal, common-sense early childhood. Much later, critics of society would equate Spock's relaxed ways with the permissiveness that spawned the lack of respect for authority seen in the 1960s and later. Nevertheless, Spock's wisdom was translated into twenty languages and had an influence far beyond U.S. shores.

The next place to feel the baby boom was the public school. Before World War II, there were few, if any, public kindergartens. They came of age in the 1950s, necessary to get the five-year-old out of the house so that his or her mother could tend to the younger children. Kindergartens moved from the basement of the town library or the city council annex to a room in one of the thousands of hastily erected public schools. Teachers no longer were mere neighbors but became credentialed experts in stacking blocks, passing out snacks, and reminding students to bring permission slips for walking trips to the fire station or the greenhouse. Nationwide public kindergartens for millions of American preschoolers represented their first attempts to socialize outside of the family.

Another school-related phenomenon caused by the huge numbers of youngsters was the teacher who also served as the principal. An ongoing shortage of teachers made running a school less crucial than having at least one accomplished adult in each classroom. Class sizes greatly exceeded those of today, and rooms with forty and even fifty kids were common. All this was done without aides, without parent volunteers, without adult crossing guards, and without paying teachers (most of whom were female) what they really were worth. It is no surprise that teachers joined unions in large numbers and became more militant as the decade wore on.

The need for more and larger schools began to affect local budgets. Property taxes always seemed a year or two behind the money needed for a costly new school or an expensive addition. The price of goods, particularly things like bricks, glass, and tile, doubled in ten years. In many cases, popular suburbs opened new schools only to find them already overcrowded! As the more successful inner-city residents moved to the suburbs, the quality of big-city schools declined. More important, the departure of people with taxable jobs meant that big-city schools were losing the means by which they could be supported. The 1950s saw the federal government come to the rescue with substantial, bipartisan-backed federal funds for education.

Fads of the Fifties

Meanwhile, elementary schoolchildren were nothing if not faddish. Davy Crockett was featured in an immensely popular Walt Disney television adventure, and boys from one end of the country to the other lustily sang the Crockett theme, "King of the Wild Frontier." Young girls became fascinated with sports heroes such as U.S. Open tennis winner Maureen ("Little Mo") Connolly or with Esther Williams, the actress who swam artistically through numerous movie musicals. Other distractions ranged from the annual baseball World Series, which was important enough to be broadcast over radios in classrooms, to electric trains, dolls, and more. In fact, any item related to kids, such as washers and dryers or baby furniture, was purchased as quickly as it could be sold all decade long.

The first wave of baby boomers became teenagers just about the time rock 'n' roll ceased to be "race music" and began to be broadcast on numer-

ous AM radio stations. Rock, said a black musician, was "white boys playing black boys' songs." Indeed it was, as Ricky Nelson sang the popular Fats Domino hit, "I'm Walkin'," so that white radio stations in the South would play the bouncy tune. Boys and girls all over the country asked for small, plug-in radios for Christmas so that they could crawl beneath the covers after lights out each night and tune in to distant stations. Powerful rock

Disney's television adaptation of Davy Crockett was immensely popular and spawned a whole range of franchised products, such as caps, shirts, and candy. Here is a 1950s' book romanticizing the life of the pioneer hero.

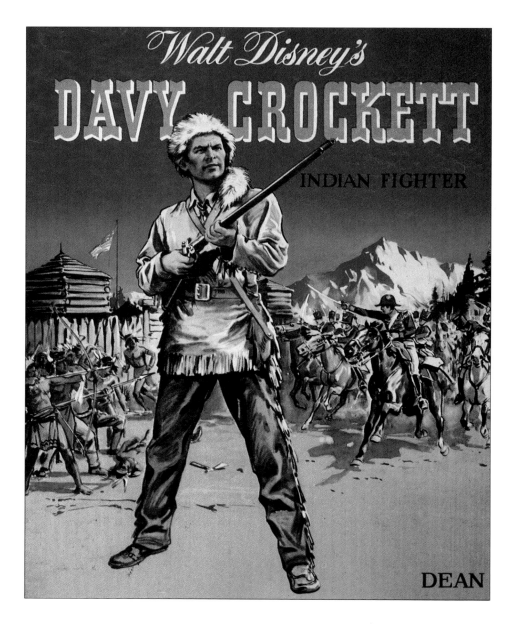

Walt Disney. (1901-1966)

Walt Disney proved conclusively in the 1950s that television was everywhere and here to stay. He did so with a weekly "Disneyland" series that included cartoons, adventures, and the exploration of nature. One adventure that helped put Disney and TV on the map was Davy Crockett.

In a series of hour-long shows, Disney told a romanticized tale of the frontiersman who died at the Alamo. Children everywhere suddenly clamored for coonskin caps and buckskin vests, eager to become little Crocketts in their backyards. There was a Davy Crockett shirt, there was Davy Crockett bubble-gum, there were Davy Crockett coloring books. The owner of several ice-cream carts in Richmond, Indiana, was unable to unload blue, popsicle-like frozen treats on the local kids until he renamed them "Davy Crockitt Popsicles." Suddenly, the sweet, drippy treats were an instant sellout.

Disney, a Chicago native, got his start by creating Mickey Mouse, the famed cartoon character, in 1928. His cartoons were crisply drawn, in black and white and then in color, and he went on to feature-length presentations such as *Snow White and the Seven Dwarfs* (1937), *Pinocchio* (1940), *Fantasia* (1940), and *Bambi* (1942). Mothers and kids were his audience before the war; postwar nature and adventure films, such as *The Living Desert* (1953) and *Davy Crockett* (1955), broadened his appeal.

So did Disneyland, one of America's top destinations during the decade. The theme park, which was scrupulously clean and offered safe rides and adventures, made Anaheim, California, a more popular destination than many national parks. Between the park, the television series, and the stream of movies and full-length cartoons, the mustachioed filmmaker created an empire.

That empire is even larger today, what with Mickey Mouse appearing on apparel and with the opening of Disney World in Florida in 1971, five years after the founder's death. The company built by Disney now is corporately owned, a huge business, and more likely to back movies closer to reality than did the operation under Walt.

Nevertheless, the man exerted a huge influence on popular culture, especially during the 1950s. He and his writers and cartoonists were able to deliver what America wanted to see and hear in the form of lighthearted entertainment as no other organization ever has.

stations in Boston, New York, Cleveland, Nashville, and Los Angeles poured out the hits, as did a young disc jockey who called himself Wolfman Jack. He furnished rock and soul music from XERF, a station just across the Texas-Mexico border, to more than half the country while peddling such items as tablecloths depicting *The Last Supper*!

In terms of style, boys combed their hair into ducktails and "flattops with fenders" as they tried to sprout Elvis Presley-type sideburns. Girls favored ponytails, though many would wind large, uncomfortable, plastic curlers called Spoolies into their hair each night before bed, hoping to emerge the next morning with a with-it style. Girls wore wooly poodle skirts and saddle shoes, boys wore jeans or pants of polished cotton. White, low-cut tennis shoes took the country by storm in the mid-1950s. Teenagers were perceived for the first time as a separate generation — they were now seen as something besides the awkward gap between a child and an adult. Consequently, the corner drug store became a soda shop, and retailers who could expect an avalanche of kids each Saturday included the record-store owner and the proprietor of the movie theater.

A Room of One's Own

By the time the first baby boomers reached puberty in the late 1950s, many of them had their own rooms — and needed them — now that children had become major consumers. Kids owned record players, records,

Portable radios meant that teenagers could groove to disk jockey Wolfman Jack or check out the latest rock 'n' roll releases in the privacy of their own rooms. This ad for the New Zenith is from 1956.

sporting goods, radios, books, and magazines. The boys often read comic books, despite the fact that the comic industry had imposed self-censorship in 1954, eliminating the very worst gore and horror. Girls had diaries, wherein they recorded each day's innermost thoughts, then locked up the poems and paragraphs with tiny keys until tomorrow. Parents indulged teenagers by creating something called a recreation room in refinished areas of the nation's basements. Card tables, ping-pong tables, pool tables, and dart boards underwent heavy use in rec rooms by millions of teenagers and their friends.

Dating revolved around school activities. Sock hops (dances) in the gymnasium following basketball or football games were common, as were formal events like proms, where athletic boys and outgoing girls were sometimes crowned kings and queens. Formal dances featured bands and orchestras, rented evening wear for the boys and pricey cocktail dresses and formals for the girls. Boys were expected to buy their dates flower corsages, which were worn to the dances, and to pay for an expensive meal at a swank restaurant sometime during the evening. If teens were apt to use alcohol, it was often on big dance nights. Beer, wine, and liquor were consumed by a few teens, who were often caught by watchful chaperones or the police. Cigarettes were the only other drug in frequent use.

Sexual Behavior

Few younger teens had sex, but the number increased as soon as most kids in a high-school class became old enough to drive. Drive-in movies,

For young people, life often revolved around the jukebox in the corner soda fountain, where they might sip a malted and swap gossip. This slice of fifties teenage life actually comes from a Broadway play of the time about the lonely child of divorced parents (rare in the fifties), called A Roomful of Roses.

lonely roads, and the family home when no one else was there became scenes of heavy petting and more. Teenage girls who became pregnant dropped out of high school to have their babies, whether they intended to keep the child or give it up for adoption. The young fathers, usually steady boyfriends, were forced to leave school, for at least a semester, as punishment for their antisocial behavior. Most females — and many males, for that matter — were virgins when they graduated high school. Speaking of virgins, that word in a script caused a 1950s movie, *The Moon is Blue*, to be censored by the motion picture industry. Times certainly have changed.

Life After High School

Most high school graduates did not go on to college during the decade. Boys realized they would be drafted by the military sooner or later and frequently enlisted for three to six years in a branch of the armed forces so that they might receive technical training and see the world. Girls who graduated from high school without college plans felt pressured to get married. They got jobs as secretaries and clerks, while non-academically minded boys signed on at local factories as hourly workers.

Typical starting pay for single high school graduates was around $2 per

Alfred C. Kinsey. (1894-1956)

Alfred Kinsey's life sounds almost like a television sitcom: The mild-mannered professor earned his degrees and studied insects until, at the age of forty-three in 1937, he was asked to teach sex education. Indiana University, where Kinsey worked in the biology department, chose him as the instructor because he was a respected biologist and a family man and the university believed it was high time students learned something about sex.

Kinsey knew little about human sexuality, and he quickly discovered that no one else knew anything, either. So he and his graduate students began vigorous investigations into who was doing what, how, and to whom. The results gained worldwide attention.

Sexual Behavior in the Human Male was published in 1948 and was followed in 1953 by *Sexual Behavior in the Human Female*. In a time when nice people seldom mentioned sex, Kinsey's scholarly research findings became bestsellers. Although the research was confined to white males and females, it did a great deal to place sexual research on the same level as any other biological inquiry.

Kinsey's findings were upsetting to some. For example, surveys of participants showed that half of all married men and one-quarter of all married women engaged in extramarital affairs. More than one-third of all males and more than 10 percent of all females had experienced homosexual excitement at some time since adolescence. Research also showed that sexual behavior differed greatly from one individual to the next and from one group to another. Despite protests by some that Kinsey and his people were obsessed with the seamier sides of sex, subsequent research has reinforced his findings.

The Kinsey reports had a liberalizing effect on sex, though they hardly can be blamed for the casual attitudes that developed in the 1960s. Indiana University's Institute for Sex Research, which the biologist founded, continues its work to this day.

INS and AP Science Writers' Review—
KINSEY BOOK ON WOMEN

hour. After taxes, these young people took home about $65 per week. Many lived at home so that their meager checks would allow them to buy a car — the ultimate status symbol for the young.

What were young people thinking? It was an era of conformity in high school and in college (vocational-technical education was unavailable for most Americans at the time). No one was very political, few people questioned authority, and only a fringe complained about things such as the radioactivity that resulted from ongoing atomic weapons testing. Beatniks, the nonconformists found in large numbers in places like New York City's Greenwich Village and in San Francisco, were idolized by a small group of teens who saw themselves as both intellectuals and outcasts. Because many were indulged by parents, they were less committed to work, less loyal to employers, and less interested in values than were their elders. When a cheating scandal hit the U.S. Military Academy at West Point, adults were shocked but most teens hardly saw it as news.

There was deep discontent among the young. Movies such as *The Blackboard Jungle* (1954) and *Rebel Without a Cause* (1955) showed kids as mixed-up, dangerous, alienated, and groping for friendship and love. The former told the story of a teacher in an inner-city school, surrounded by tough kids, who was trying to make a difference. The violence on the screen was accompanied by violence in theaters where the film was shown. To the movie theme of *Rock Around the Clock,* teenage viewers cut up seats, fought each other with fists and knives, and caused several theaters to close immediately. *Rebel Without a Cause* showed a high school loner, played by James Dean, who was misunderstood by his uncaring parents and by a school filled with angry and hostile students and remote teachers. Both films had huge teenage followings.

The Silent Generation

If teenagers were boisterous, college students were almost inaudible. Terribly serious, they looked down their noses at protest, dissent, and nonconformity. Numbering more than 3.5 million by the late 1950s, they were conservative politically, religiously, and personally. Most believed that persons accused of crimes should be deprived of their rights when necessary, felt that "going steady" was preferable to dating around, and the majority attended church on a regular basis or admitted to having strong mainline Protestant or Roman Catholic religious beliefs. When they played, they went to sporting events, drank beer and ate pizza, danced, went skiing, went to the movies, and listened to music. Most intended to be Republicans because they believed that was wanted by the corporations they hoped would hire them. Frequently, the only questioning voice in the college classroom belonged to the instructor.

A Young Rebel

How did it happen, then, that the decade's most popular literary figure was a rebel? His name was Holden Caulfield, a teenager who skipped out of prep school to loiter in New York, and he is as important a character as there is in twentieth-century American literature. Caulfield was the troubled, introspective hero of J. D. Salinger's *Catcher in the Rye,* a slim novel that continues to sell by the millions and is read by high school and college students to this day. Salinger joined the giants of earlier decades on the bookshelves of college dormitories everywhere. He was much more popular among the young than other promising post-World War II authors, including John Cheever, James Jones, Norman Mailer, and John Updike. Not that this was a literary age — television was in virtually every home by the end of the decade, as most Americans set aside books and newspapers, puzzles, and games to be bathed in the daily and nightly glow of the picture-filled box.

"I keep picturing all these little kids in this big field of rye. . . . If they're running and they don't look where they're going I have to come out from somewhere and catch them. That's all I'd do all day. I'd just be the catcher in the rye. I know it's crazy."

Catcher in the Rye,
J.D. Salinger, 1951

(Opposite) In this obviously posed picture, three young fifties women feign shock and surprise at a newspaper review of the Kinsey report on sexual behaviour in women. The work was a serious study but its topic titillated the public and it became a bestseller.

CHAPTER 4
Returning to God

The Sunday morning was a warm one and the 1950s Venice, Florida, family wasn't in the mood to dress up — though they would have felt guilty had they missed church. So they threw on shorts and T-shirts and hopped into the family Studebaker, heading for a nearby drive-in movie. Greeted at the gate by a fellow Presbyterian, they were invited to park in any row. Dad hung the speaker on the car door, and they all heard a heartfelt sermon. Communion took place up near the bottom of the big screen, but those unable or unwilling to leave their coupes and sedans were brought tiny paper cups filled with grape juice. Religion, show business, and the automobile all met on shimmering Florida asphalt that summer morning.

Even among today's Americans, used to drive-up windows at restau-rants, banks, and dry cleaners, the church service at a drive-in movie may strike them as strange. First of all, drive-in theaters have all but disappeared from the American landscape. They took up too much room in places where developers wanted to build offices, homes, and strip malls on valu-able real estate. Second, now that reli-gion is a cable television fixture on many different channels, families can tune in at home and feel almost blessed, even if they fail to take communion. And third, religion in the 1990s is far different from religion in the 1950s.

Religions Grow and Prosper

The spiritual revival of the 1950s buoyed religion, especially Christiani-

In the fifties, devout Christianity was a firm sign of anticommunism and many made a public show of attending church to avoid suspicion. Here, more than a thousand students at the University of Notre Dame fill the Sacred Heart Church on campus, in November 1956, in a "prayerful protest" against the Soviet use of force to crush the Hungarian rebellion. The university's student senate sponsored the group prayer service.

Evangelism attracted many supporters in the fifties. Here, the Reverend Milton Perry, a twenty-three-year-old Harlem evangelist, leads a follower with upraised arms to receive God at an evangelistic rally in New York, in 1957. The Rev. Perry claimed that around 300 lame, blind, and crippled people had been "cured" in his revival tent.

ty, as no revival had since the days of Billy Sunday and Amy Semple Mc-Pherson in the 1920s. In 1940, for example, less than half the population belonged to a church of any kind. By the time the fifties revival crested late in the decade, more than 63 percent listed themselves as church members. Unlike earlier revivals, this one affected all classes of society. It also affected pocketbooks: Religious contributions reached a record $3.4 billion in 1957, enabling many denominations to build large and elaborate new houses of worship. There were even door-to-door Bible salespeople, many of whom made decent livings.

Americans today are much less judgmental about different religions than they were thirty or forty years earlier. Back then, certain religions called mainline denominations were the only ones "approved" by the middle- and upper-class white members of the community. These faiths included Baptists, Episcopalians, Lutherans, Methodists, Presbyterians, and most other denominations that were members of the National Council of Churches. Frowned upon by mainline Christians were Pentecostals, Fundamentalists, various "holy rollers," and other more vividly emotional, less stuffy denominations attended by working-class white people and by blacks, each in their own houses of worship. The sons and daughters of these committed people would grow up and multiply, often luring numerous sons and daughters of traditional Protestant churches into born-again, back-to-God, hellfire-and-brimstone, absolute, back-to-the-Bible Christianity. But not in the 1950s.

Catholicism in America

In the decade before John F. Kennedy, America's first Catholic president, was elected to office, members of his religious faith were still viewed with suspicion by the ruling Protestant majority. These altar boys are attending Mass at St. Vincent Ferrer R.C. Church.

Also looked at with skepticism by the white power structure were the innumerable Roman Catholics, who were sometimes thought of as Catholics first and Americans second. These descendants of the Irish and southern and eastern European immigrants seemed "just like us," the mainliners felt, except they usually attended their own schools, were taught by nuns, and were more apt to actually show up in church every Sunday than their Protestant counterparts. Likewise, Jews, Unitarians, Quakers, and others seen as nonmainstream were mistrusted, but not as much as atheists, who were consistently equated with Communists. A rather unconventional

dean of women at a state college in West Virginia was dismissed from her position in 1952 "for being an atheist who didn't believe in God." The woman sued for slander but was given only money in compensation rather than her former job.

Meanwhile, across the Atlantic Ocean, events were taking place that would deeply affect the fifty million Roman Catholics who were U.S. citizens. Pope Pius XII died in October 1958 in Rome's Vatican City. He was succeeded by Pope John XXIII, a plump, seventy-seven-year-old cardinal regarded by many as someone with low energy who would serve only briefly. Instead, John called for the Second Vatican Council, which would, in the 1960s, alter the way Catholics looked at the church, their

country, and themselves. Among those who took little note of the election was a young Irish-American politician, an Ivy Leaguer, a war hero, and the son of one of the most powerful men in America. That man was U.S. Senator John F. Kennedy, who would play down the fact that he was Catholic and play up the fact that he was an American in his successful 1960 presidential bid.

Religion in Popular Culture

Another older person who exerted real religious influence was a movie director by the name of Cecil B. De Mille. Born in Massachusetts in 1881, De Mille put out a number of films with religious themes, the most important being *The Ten Commandments*, which he made twice, in 1923 and again in 1956. The latter movie was more than three hours long and took the better part of a year to make. It starred Charlton Heston as Moses and Yul Brynner as the Egyptian ruler, Rameses. Heston also starred in William Wyler's biblical epic, *Ben Hur*, in 1959. That was the year De Mille died, having contributed tales of sin and redemption to the screen and conceived vast landscapes with casts of thousands. Even the most casual American believer was swept up in such colorful dramas.

Popular songs with religious themes were heard every day on the radio. Before rock 'n' roll overwhelmed the singing of ballads, tunes like "I

Religion was also manifested in the many epic movies made in the fifties. Here, Charlton Heston can be seen battling it out in the famous chariot race scene from Ben Hur *in 1959.*

Methodist minister Norman Vincent Peale communicated largely though his writings and a network radio program named "The Art of Living." He also hosted a popular television program "What's Your Problem?" in the sixties and became president of the Reformed Church of America, making him one of the most familiar clergymen in America.

Believe," "It Is No Secret What God Can Do," and "Vaya Con Dios," all made the Lucky Strike cigarette-sponsored "Hit Parade," a weekly television show that reviewed the most popular music in the country. The words "under God" were added by Congress to the Pledge of Allegiance, and schools preceded athletic events, assemblies, and graduations with either a prayer or a moment of silence. In 1956, a Presbyterian minister in New York City conceived Dial-A-Prayer.

Callers to the widely publicized number would receive a devotional message that changed every day. Such phone services became common in larger cities all across the country.

Religion conquered the bestsellers book list, too. The second most successful book of 1952 was *A Man Called Peter,* by Catherine Marshall. It told the story of Marshall's husband, who served as the chaplain in the U.S. Senate until his death. By the time the book-based movie was produced in 1955, the nonfiction work had sold more than 1.5 million copies. *The Revised Standard Version of the Bible* turned up on bestseller lists for several years during the fifties, and so did several books with a strong religious flavor. *The Reader's Digest* successfully condensed *The Bible,* apparently for persons who felt religious but who were pressed for time. Other popular books included *Peace of Mind* by Joshua Loth Liebman, a Jew, and *The Power of Positive Thinking* by Dr. Norman Vincent Peale, a Methodist.

Peale, Graham, and Sheen

The Rev. Dr. Peale, together with the Rev. Billy Graham and Bishop Fulton J. Sheen, represented religion to an overwhelming number of Americans in the 1950s. The Methodist Peale got rich peddling *Guideposts,* a religious magazine with eight hundred thousand readers. He also sold books and greeting cards, wrote a column for *Look* magazine, and was named one of the twelve best U.S. salesmen in 1954. Peale's message was a reassuring combination of religion, success stories, and comfort. He urged thinking positive thoughts and eliminating negative

thinking, concepts that probably aided the religious and nonreligious alike. Peale stayed away from political topics until 1960, when he openly opposed John F. Kennedy's presidential run because Kennedy was Catholic.

Billy Graham was a plain-talking Fundamentalist minister who attracted large crowds attended by flashy and talented singers and by followers willing to spread the word that the Rev. Graham was coming to town. Graham's fame really began following a large revival in Los Angeles, and he became known internationally following a religious crusade to Britain. His message was simple and not always easy to accept: The end is coming, so we had better be prepared. Graham frowned on social activism, believing strongly in faith but not in good works. He told listeners that they were discontented not for external, social reasons but because they had a bad relationship with God. He was a regular visitor to the White House and met with congressional leaders over prayer breakfasts. Two of Graham's books, *Peace With God* (1953) and *The Secret of Happiness* (1955), became bestsellers.

Graham turned up with increasing frequency on television and so did Bishop Sheen. Sheen was the host of "Life Is Worth Living," broadcast nationally from 1952 to 1957. The thirty-minute program, which competed with comedian Milton Berle on another network, covered many topics. But his most wrathful shows involved communism and its hazards for America. He warned that commies were seeping into schools, colleges, and government, and in a 1953 television broadcast, he warned Josef Stalin that the Soviet dictator would soon have to answer to God. Stalin died almost immediately after that, and

many Americans wondered if the bishop had some sort of divine vision. At the height of his popularity, Bishop Sheen enjoyed an audience of ten million viewers.

While Billy Graham was the only evangelist with a mainline, middle-class following, there were hundreds of other evangelists who traveled around the country, praying, healing, singing, motivating, and asking for money to continue the religious fervor. These people, almost all of whom were men, seemed to originate in the South, which has always been more religious than the rest of the country. Among the most prominent was Oral Roberts from Oklahoma. He was a Penetecostal Holiness preacher and a faith healer who built an empire, despite the fact that at least two women whom he said were cured of cancer and diabetes quickly died after being treated by him. By the end of the decade, his weekly service was on four hundred television stations.

If the average American believed that Christian evangelists were indeed "holy rollers," he or she was at least as skeptical of minority and non-Christian religions. Jews felt the wrath of the majority every time the Middle East erupted, such as in 1956 when Israel invaded Egypt's Sinai peninsula. Quakers and other pacifists were viewed as misguided, as were such fringe strains of mainline religions like the Catholic Workers. The latter organization, which ran a mission for homeless persons in the Bowery section of New York City, was eyed with suspicion, despite the fact that it fed more than three hundred down-and-out people every day for twenty-one years. Religious congregations with foreign roots, such as Islam, Buddhism, or Hinduism, were common

Billy Graham.

Billy Graham greatly broadened the appeal of Christian evangelism — or preaching the gospel in order to convert or return people to the faith. Brought up as a strict Presbyterian in Charlotte, North Carolina, Graham was ordained a Southern Baptist in 1939 and graduated from Wheaton College in 1943. From 1943 to 1946, he was the pastor of a Baptist church in west suburban Chicago. He also joined an organization called Youth for Christ International.

Beginning in 1946, Billy Graham turned to evangelism. He startled the country with a simple, direct, and dramatic form of preaching that had seldom been heard. In contrast to the frequently obscure or theatrical or befuddling messages of other evangelist preachers, Graham was easy to understand. With the assistance of a professional team of singers and organizers, he filled huge churches and stadiums, first in the U.S. and then all around the world.

Supported initially by fundamental Baptists, Graham came to be enjoyed by members of all major Christian denominations. He launched the Billy Graham Evangelistic Association in 1950, crusading in many major cities before taking his message to Europe. In London, he won not only all of the Baptists but also everyone from the Archbishop of Canterbury to the head of religious programming for BBC radio broadcasting. Clearly, he was an exceptional orator.

Graham became a familiar face on television. Millions watched his crusades, admiring his scrupulous honesty. He displayed aggression only when talking about sin. He not only recruited thousands but also paved the way for a whole generation of television evangelists to come — not all of whom were as pious as he. Not even close friendship with President Richard M. Nixon (who later resigned) in the early 1970s could sully the Christian preacher's longstanding, worldwide, positive reputation.

Despite some physical problems, Graham continues to preach and write. His best-known book, *Peace With God*, was published in 1953 and details his faith and beliefs.

only in the nation's largest cities.

Women sought more important roles in religion with varying degrees of success. The most well-known female theologian of the decade was Georgia Harkness, who taught at the Pacific School of Religion in California. The three books she wrote during the decade were a call to the average woman in the congregation to use her uniquely feminine social gifts for the greater good. Methodists ordained their first female minister in 1951, while Mary Lyman was ordained a Congregational minister a year earlier. Lyman also worked for the advancement of the National Council of Churches, writing a popular religious work in 1956 titled *Into All the World*.

Religion and Civil Rights

Perhaps the most courageous religious woman was Dorothy Rogers Tilly, a white southern woman and a

Martin Luther King, Jr. (1929-1968)

Though he is usually perceived as a man of the 1960s, Martin Luther King, Jr., laid important groundwork for social change a decade earlier. Born the son of a Baptist minister and a schoolteacher, King enrolled at Morehouse College in Atlanta in 1944. There, he was influenced by Dr. Benjamin Mays, a scholar whose religious convictions convinced King that he could be fulfilled in the ministry.

The Atlanta native went on to a theological seminary and then completed work for his doctorate. King returned to the South a forceful speaker, accepting a job as pastor at the Dexter Avenue Baptist Church in Montgomery, Alabama. From his pulpit, he helped mobilize fellow African-Americans in the 382-day boycott of the city's public bus system. King and his family survived the bombing of his home and he recovered from his arrest before the U.S. Supreme Court ruled that blacks could ride Montgomery buses on an equal footing with white passengers.

With that triumph over segregation, in 1957 King called together various African-American leaders to form the Southern Christian Leadership Conference. It was an activist, religiously oriented civil rights group, and he was elected its president. The organization gained fame throughout the South for its voter registration drives and its protests against discrimination.

Dr. King left the United States briefly in 1960, after completing his first book. He traveled to India to study the kind of nonviolent civil disobedience that had been practiced so successfully by Mohandas Gandhi. He returned to the scene of his greatest triumph — a mass protest in Birmingham, Alabama, which resulted in the desegregation of most public places and the start of fair-hiring policies. Although he was jailed, he communicated with his followers by letter, including a classic defense of integration in his "Letter from a Birmingham Jail."

A hypnotic speaker, King's finest hour took place in 1963. He and others organized a massive March on Washington. A crowd of thousands heard him deliver his "I have a dream" speech, which envisioned equality and harmony between the races. *Time* magazine named him Man of the Year for 1963. Even more important, he was named the recipient of the 1964 Nobel Peace Prize. That same year, he led the Selma-to-Montgomery Freedom March to advocate black voter registration.

Aways maintaining a clear overview of the country's problems, King attacked the United States for being at war in Vietnam. He tied this huge expense in human lives and materials to the War on Poverty, pointing out that the latter was the battle that should be fought. Such views brought rallies, boycotts, dissents, and the willingness to go to jail to the antiwar movement. Among a huge number of Americans, King's message was as vital as ever. King's birthday, January 15, is now a national holiday.

Methodist. In an age when there weren't many civil rights reformers, at least among middle-class whites, she formed a group she called the Fellowship of the Concerned. This organization spoke out against segregation, despite threats from Ku Klux Klansmen and varying degrees of outrage from friends and acquaintances. Tilly enlisted four thousand members in her organization, while another white woman, Virginia Foster Durr, worked with religious organizations and the National Association for the

Advancement of Colored People (NAACP) to help bring peaceful integration to Alabama.

A More Religious President

Dwight Eisenhower was not a particularly religious man. Before becoming president, he had no religious preference, and he did not go to church. All that changed once he was in office: Ike quickly became a Presbyterian following the 1952 election. When asked about his faith, the president usually offered a pleasant mixture of feelings about God, Christ, prayer, and being an American. He usually went to church every Sunday, though he occasionally skipped on sunny mornings for a round of golf. Cabinet meetings began either with a silent prayer or with a prayer offered by Ezra Taft Benson, the secretary of agriculture and a Mormon. The president's attitude toward faith mirrored the country's.

Eisenhower was a joiner — why else stay with an army that, between World War I and World War II, lost most of its manpower and was weaker in 1938 than it had been in 1918? The country was also full of joiners, and many of the organizations people got involved in were related to their church. And why not? Churches gave people a sense of community, a sense of belonging. People taught Sunday school, served as lay people during the service, raised money by cooking for chili suppers and pancake breakfasts, visited shut-in members, contributed to church, served on the board that assisted the pastor and ran the individual church, and made plans for an addition or for a newer and bigger church as people had more children and membership increased.

A Poor Understanding

For all their religion, surveys showed that Americans were incredibly ignorant about Christianity. A 1951 Gallup Poll indicated that more than half of Christians queried could not name one of the gospels. Few Protestants understood or were able to explain the concept of the trinity, and their shallow approach was reinforced by numerous pastors who endorsed Hollywood religious movies as a way to learn the faith. Most who saw *The Ten Commandments* called it "a moving religious experience." If art became pop in the 1960s, pop religion was everywhere a decade earlier. In fact, an astounding 95 percent of Americans contacted in a survey claimed to be religious.

It would be cruel to call this great religious revival a fad, but that must have been partly what it was. Like the great surges of American religious popularity in the eighteenth and nineteenth centuries, it ebbed and flowed before peaking, this time in the mid-1950s. Church membership began a long and slow decline after that, perhaps in part because people were learning to live with the threats of communism and atomic weapons. Despite the fact that President Eisenhower had sent a few military advisors to help the South Vietnamese, Americans believed the next war was a long way off. After all, hadn't the U.S. declined to participate in a British action involving the Suez Canal in 1956? Perhaps those Sundays spent in church by the president instead of on the golf course were paying dividends.

CHAPTER 5
Racial Confrontations and Civil Rights

Elizabeth Eckford wasn't the kind of teenager who normally attracted attention. But she was the focus of millions of Americans on that early-September day in 1957. Eckford was the first black student to enter all-white Central High School in Little Rock, Arkansas. Television cameras recorded the jeers of white students and adults as Elizabeth attempted to enter the school past the Arkansas National Guardsmen who had been stationed there. The Arkansas governor, Orville Faubus, had warned that there would be trouble if blacks were admitted to the big public school. He did so in part because he was up for reelection and knew that an anti-integration stance would win him votes. His dire predictions encouraged confrontation.

Eisenhower wasn't looking for a fight. He had completed the desegregation of the armed services started by his predecessor, Harry S Truman, but Ike was no progressive when it came to matters of race. He successfully nominated Earl Warren of California as chief justice of the U.S. Supreme Court, then condemned Warren after the high court decided, in 1954, in *Brown v. the Board of Education of Topeka, Kansas,* that separate facilities for blacks didn't make those facilities equal according to the Constitution. Because of the decision, schools and other public institutions everywhere, but particularly in the South, were forced to take steps to integrate.

Integration had taken place a year earlier, amid rock throwing and name calling, at the University of Alabama in Tuscaloosa. There, a black woman named Autherine Lucy successfully enrolled under the watchful eyes of federal marshals and armed forces. (Lucy was later expelled for having made "baseless allegations" against college authorities!) In Louisiana, Governor Earl Long endorsed state legislation that made the social mixing of races — even in athletic contests — illegal. Though there were troubles in 1957 in a few other towns and cities in Kentucky, Tennessee, and Texas, school integration took place quietly in many southern states. But not in Arkansas.

Elizabeth Eckford calmly ignores the taunts of fellow pupil Hazel Bryant (center background with her mouth open) and others at Little Rock Central High School in Arkansas, as she tries to gain entrance to the school in 1957. Elizabeth was the first black student in the all-white school. This was among the first of many confrontations across the South, as the region took on the federal government over the segregation issue.

"Bloodshed and Mob Violence"

The sign that says it all. John Carter, aged seventeen, displays a placard outside his high school in Clinton, Tennessee, protesting against enforced racial integration in August 1956. Carter and a few of the other 750 students at the school refused to enter the building now that African-Americans had joined the previously all-white classes. Integration began under order of a federal court, despite its rejection by the Clinton school board.

A group calling itself the League of Central High School Mothers sought a court order to prevent the admission of black children. Their effort succeeded because the mothers' chief witness was Governor Faubus. He forecast "bloodshed and mob violence," persuading the court to delay integration. A higher court quickly overruled matters, and Faubus declared a state of emergency. He called out two hundred Arkansas National Guard members to prevent nine black children from entering school on September 3. When inte-grationists smuggled the nine into the school through a side door, three hundred white students streamed out the front. Many of the whites still inside taunted the black students until they were taken back to their homes in police cars at noon.

President Eisenhower reacted slowly but with force. He sent a thousand paratroopers to cordon off the streets around the school. Noting that it was "a sad day," the popular chief executive could have marshaled public opinion had he spoken out earlier or more strongly. Meanwhile, Americans saw on their television sets that the black children looked scared and innocent carrying their books and lunches, while the whites being held back by troops acted ignorant and unruly. TV was quietly molding opinion while Eisenhower's elite troops stayed in Little Rock until Thanksgiving — two days after Ike suffered a stroke that left him temporarily unable to speak.

The South, Then and Now

Looking back on the beginnings of racial integration, it's easy to make false assumptions. The average southern white resident was neither ignorant nor blindly bigoted. Rather, he or she disliked outsiders tinkering with the roots of a civilization that had been humiliated a century earlier in the Civil War and was about to be humiliated again. Jim Crow laws, passed decades earlier to keep the races separated, were being picked apart by the federal courts. Southerners were deeply religious, even more so than other Americans in the 1950s, and they felt that the judiciary was upsetting God's natural order — the way

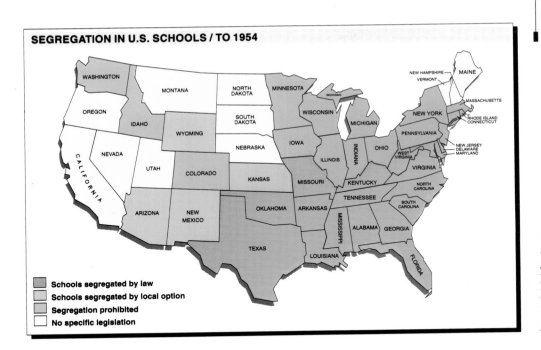

SEGREGATION IN U.S. SCHOOLS / TO 1954

■ Schools segregated by law
□ Schools segregated by local option
■ Segregation prohibited
□ No specific legislation

This map shows the states that embraced school segregation before the 1954 Brown v. the Board of Education Supreme Court ruling that declared the practice illegal.

things were meant to be. White people believed blacks to be naturally inferior. So when white extremists balked at integration, many otherwise reasonable people fell in with them.

How divided was the South before racial integration? The races did not mix on athletic fields, in movie theaters, in churches, in swimming pools, at drinking fountains, in doctors' offices, in hospitals, in orphanages, or in libraries. African-Americans were prevented from casting votes in several ways: They were charged money called poll taxes; they were given tests no one could pass; and they were put on endless waiting lists. Even those who somehow paid the fees and passed the tests were simply told not to vote if they wanted to live. Public transportation was segregated, too, with rear seats reserved for blacks — unless there were too many whites, in which case blacks were expected to stand. All that began to change in 1955, in Montgomery, Alabama, deep in the heart of Dixie.

Boycotting Montgomery's Buses

The Montgomery chapter of the National Association for the Advancement of Colored People (NAACP) had been looking for ways to confront the city. An opportunity arose in 1955, when an African-American woman named Rosa Parks refused to give up her seat on a local public bus so a white person could sit down. Parks was arrested and taken to jail, even though the woman later indicated that she refused to move simply because she was tired. Black leaders meeting in churches throughout the city called for a boycott of the bus system. Among those leaders was a young minister named Martin Luther King, Jr.

King served the Dexter Avenue Baptist Church, in Montgomery. From his pulpit, he and other leaders preached nonviolent behavior as a way of fighting the white power structure. Blacks ceased riding Montgomery

"The South stands at Armageddon. . . . We cannot make the slightest concession to the enemy in this dark and lamentable hour of struggle. There is no more difference in compromising the integrity of race on the playing field than in doing so in the classroom."

Georgia Governor Marvin Griffin, on the Supreme Court *Brown v. Board of Education* decision, 1954

buses, car-pooling wherever possible, and walking when no ride presented itself. The buses ran their routes virtually empty, causing the city to lose money to transport a small number of white riders. The bus boycott lasted more than a year before city officials accepted a court order that integrated public transportation. Martin Luther King, Jr., emerged from the ordeal as the nation's most famous civil rights activist.

The boycotters paid a dear price for their determination. They were beaten, their homes and churches were bombed, and they were jailed. They received little encouragement from the federal government, where people like FBI Director J. Edgar Hoover called nonviolent resistance "a pernicious doctrine." But King had

Rosa Parks.

Rosa Parks, a seamstress, was tired on that December evening in 1955 when she boarded the Cleveland Avenue bus in Montgomery, Alabama. An African-American, she sat down heavily with a small bag of groceries in the middle section of the bus.

The bus began to fill with black and white people. A local law dictated that black riders must give up their seats and stand in the rear of the bus whenever white people could not find a seat. When a white rider asked for Rosa's seat, she refused, remaining seated until her arrest several hours later. Her refusal was the beginning of a civil rights era that changed American history forever.

Prior to her arrest, Parks had been active in the Montgomery chapter of the National Association for the Advancement of Colored People (NAACP). Born in rural Montgomery County, she had received a decent education at a local parochial school for African-American girls run by the Congregational church. She later married Raymond Parks, a barber, and worked as a file clerk in an insurance firm and then as a department store seamstress before the bus incident.

Actually, the refusal had grown out of work Parks and E. D. Nixon, a black union leader, had begun a bit earlier. Nixon had tried without success to convince local white bus drivers that they should treat African-American riders with more respect. After Parks' arrest, blacks began a boycott of the city's public transportation system. In 1956, the U.S. Supreme Court ruled that Alabama's state and local laws regarding bus segregation were illegal.

In the meantime, Parks had been fired from her job. She and her husband moved to Virginia, where they both found new jobs. They later moved to Detroit so that Rosa could work for twenty-five years as a special assistant to a congressman. Parks still lives in Michigan, where she is founder and president of the Rosa and Raymond Parks Institute for Self-Development.

The impact of the bus boycott and the court ruling began a wave of civil disobedience by blacks all across the American South. The civil rights movement mobilized and unified blacks and sympathetic whites as nothing had before. One by one, schools, lunch counters, motels, and country clubs all across the land became truly open to the entire public, black or white, for the first time.

studied the writings and activities of historic pacifists such as America's Henry David Thoreau and India's Mohandas Gandhi. He blended their thinking with Christian Fundamentalism to convince his followers that they were morally right and that they would eventually triumph.

White Supremacist Organizations

As black people throughout the South became better organized, so did whites who opposed integration. The Ku Klux Klan (KKK), formed during Civil War Reconstruction to keep African-Americans in their place, enjoyed a revival in the 1920s and again in the 1950s. KKK members usually were rural, ill-educated, south-

ern white men who hid their identities behind sheets, burned crosses as symbols of resistance, and used violence whenever nothing else worked. Two things kept the Klan from becoming more than an irregular factor in the move toward an integrated society: First, the organization split into more than a dozen organizations that competed for membership. Second, most white southerners who felt strongly about race joined the White Citizens' Councils, which sprang up all over the South. The councils tended to fight desegregation without resorting to violence, using state and local laws to deprive African-Americans of their rights.

Nevertheless, Klan units stretched from North Carolina to Texas and as far north as Indiana. Members often were unemployed outcasts who feared

> "Many unconsciously wondered if they deserved better conditions. Their minds were so conditioned to segregation that they submissively adjusted to things as they were. This is the ultimate tragedy of segregation."
>
> Martin Luther King, Jr., 1956

black access to blue-collar and agricultural jobs and believed that they were protecting Christianity, their sisters, and the white race. The Klan's view of the world would evolve after the 1950s into survivalist and other white, Christian, militant organizations that stockpiled weapons and supplies and either waited or hoped for the world to end.

The Klan suffered a number of setbacks in the 1950s. After several Klansmen kidnaped and tortured a black man in Birmingham, Alabama, in 1957 as part of an initiation, they expected him to die. But he lived to testify against the group, each of whom received twenty-year prison terms in a southern court. In 1958, the KKK was humiliated on film that ran on network television news. Staging a show to prove the superiority of white persons over a North Carolina tribe of American Indians, the Klansmen ran for their lives, sheets flapping, when the natives took offense. Yet the Klansmen were taken seriously, primarily because they bombed everything from integrated YMCAs to churches and synagogues.

African-American Concerns

Perhaps because they were America's largest minority, blacks got a growing amount of attention during the 1950s. This may have happened because of the degree of unity they enjoyed. A 1957 Gallup Poll, for example, showed that 69 percent of African-Americans residing in the South favored the 1954 U.S. Supreme Court decision outlawing "separate but equal facilities." Most blacks — and a growing number of whites outside the South — endorsed nonviolent

actions, such as boycotts, to achieve equality. Federal lawmakers probably sensed the mood in Washington, D.C., when they passed the Civil Rights Act of 1957. The first such legislation in eighty-two years, the act was initiated by the Eisenhower administration and was aimed at righting racial inequities. Despite attempts to block the bill, it passed — after sixty-three days of rancorous debate!

The bill, despite being watered down, set several important standards. First, it set up a Civil Rights Division within the Department of Justice. Although this unit would not make headlines until several years later, its existence was an important step. Second, it gave the U.S. attorney general the power to obtain court injunctions against persons attempting to deprive others of their voting rights. Third, it created a Commission on Civil Rights to study the entire question. The bill was not vigorously enforced, but it contained seeds that would sprout into a real commitment to enforcing minorities' civil rights later on.

Often, ordinary citizens were far ahead of the federal government in matters of civil rights. In 1958, for example, some ten thousand young people from all across the country staged a march on Washington, demanding an end to segregation.

Other Minorities

Reading 1950s newspaper headlines, an American might think the country had only one minority group. Other minorities had other problems, no less important to them than were civil rights to blacks. American Indian children, on or off the reservation, were sent mixed messages. Were they to honor their traditional ways and live apart from society or participate fully in American life and lose their heritage in the process? Mexican-Americans, many of whom lived in Texas and California, were discriminated against or simply ignored. Farm workers, whether foreigners admitted to harvest crops or native-born, suffered from overwork, low pay, and harsh conditions in the fields. White people in California hired Hispanics in large numbers only for housework, gardening, and other manual tasks.

When Alaska and Hawaii became the forty-ninth and fiftieth states in 1959, it presented problems and opportunities for Inuit (Eskimos) and American Indians in Alaska and for Hawaiians and Japanese-Americans in the Hawaiian islands. Other groups, such as the Amish, were under pressure to school their children in public facilities as educational rules became more uniform and less flexible across the country.

Media Stereotypes

If television played a role in bringing equality to the United States, it also provided many scenes in the 1950s that resulted in distorted or stereotyped views of minorities. Perhaps the most famous minority representative on television in the 1950s was Tonto, the Lone Ranger's obedient sidekick. But there were many others. Millions saw Chinese as wise and crafty, thanks to broadcasts of Charlie Chan detective movies. They laughed at a character named Jose

While white middle-class Americans enjoyed all the trappings of postwar prosperity, there were many other families living in the U.S. whose lives could not have been more different. This Creek Indian family has no choice but to live in destitution at a migrant workers' camp. Walter Lena plays jump rope in the dust with daughter Shirley, while his wife Stella sits outside their shack with the baby.

Jimenez, played by comedian Bill Dana on "The Steve Allen Show." Viewers were also offered many opportunities for a distorted view of African-Americans, as "The Amos 'n' Andy Show" became popular and as children's shows such as "Ramar of the Jungle" showed a smart white man leading a group of not-so-smart black men. Contributing further to stereotypes was the fact that the only other black people shown on TV were singers, dancers, musicians, and athletes.

Television wasn't the only culprit. Newspapers large and small simply neglected daily life in minority communities. The only minorities who made news anywhere besides the sports pages were criminals. Those who led law-abiding lives were lucky to get their names in print when they were born, when they were married, or when they died. Radio was equally slanted or negligent. However, several big cities were able to support minority-owned and -focused daily or weekly newspapers and radio stations. Black radio stations played gospel and blues music, which became mainstream rock 'n' roll during the decade.

In the South, books on the evils of integration, sometimes masked as

Children were exposed to racial stereotypes at an early age thanks to TV series like "The Lone Ranger," which premiered in 1949. American Indian Jay Silverheels played the downtrodden and obsequious Tonto to Clayton Moore's all knowing Lone Ranger.

Paul Robeson. (1898-1976)

Paul Robeson's story is a familiar one. In order to receive the recognition he deserved, he had to be twice as good as the competition, simply because he was black. Fortunately for Robeson, he was very good.

The son of a slave who became a minister, he graduated first in his college class at Rutgers University in 1918, earning Phi Beta Kappa honors. He then graduated with honors from Columbia University's law school in 1923. Yet he did not practice the law. Possessed of a wonderful voice, Robeson became a professional singer and an actor, giving concerts that showcased his bass voice. He made popular several Negro spirituals and immortalized "Ol' Man River," from the musical, *Showboat.* His career also was tied to the rendering of such rousing labor songs as "Joe Hill."

His magnetic presence on a stage made up for the fact that he was only an average actor. Many roles seemed made for him, from Eugene O'Neill's *The Emperor Jones* to William Shakespeare's *Othello.* Unfortunately for Robeson, he became fascinated with the Russian language. That led to a visit to the Soviet Union in the 1930s and his support of the Communist line thereafter, even though he did not join the party itself. J. Edgar Hoover, director of the Federal Bureau of Investigation, tormented the singer for the rest of his days for having said kind things about the Soviets. Robeson and his wife were summoned before congressional committees in the 1950s to explain themselves. For several years, he was not permitted to travel abroad, and such harmless events as a large birthday celebration were infiltrated with government agents who scanned the crowd for spies and subversives! Many friends were afraid to be seen with him.

Robeson did not handle the shadowing and harassment well, suffering several breakdowns and becoming addicted to prescription drugs. His support of all things Soviet was naive, but he certainly deserved better treatment than he received, as did many others during these years of Communist witch hunts.

political studies on the rights of individual states, were common. So were purportedly scientific books and articles that "proved" black people needed to be overseen by whites. Yet one book, published in 1960 but researched during the late 1950s, overwhelmed anything else in print. Titled *Black Like Me,* this diarylike work of nonfiction was written by a white author, John Howard Griffith, who shaved his straight hair and worked with a dermatologist to alter the color of his skin. He traveled throughout the South for just six weeks, suffering racial slurs, being refused service at restaurants, and experiencing other humiliations. This moving account would serve as a preview of the resistance to civil rights in the 1960s and the many successes enjoyed by African-Americans at last.

CHAPTER 6
Surviving the Cold War

On a sunny spring day in 1950, a police officer in Wheeling, West Virginia, stopped in a neighborhood store to buy a pack of Lucky Strikes. On his way out, he stopped at the row of candy and gumball machines lined up next to the door and noticed a new one that claimed to dispense a mini-geography lesson *and* a piece of candy for each penny inserted. What a great idea for kids, he thought. He slipped a penny into the slot and gave the lever a half turn to release a gumball, then carefully unwrapped it to read the geography lesson.

What he read absolutely appalled him. The scrap of paper clearly showed the Soviet flag with its hammer and sickle and the statistics: "USSR. Population: 211,000,000. Capital: Moscow. Largest country in the world." Feeling sick, the officer pocketed the evidence and walked the six blocks to the city manager's office. Robert Plummer, city manager, gave the matter top priority and immediately arranged to have the offensive candy machines removed from every store in the city — to protect innocent children from knowledge of that Communist stronghold, the Soviet Union. "This is a terrible thing to expose our children to," he was quoted as saying.

This bizarre incident was hardly an isolated case. Haunted by the terrors of the Cold War and the nuclear arms race, Americans in the fifties were terrified of a Communist takeover, even though the U.S. was now undeniably the world's most powerful and prosperous nation.

The Witch Hunt for Communists Begins

After World War II, many Republicans took advantage of the Red Scare by accusing the Democrats (especially those in Truman's administration) of selling out to the Russians. These suspicions increased in 1948 when a long-time State Department official named Alger Hiss was accused of passing important State Department documents to Russian agents back in the late 1930s. Hiss denied all the charges and claimed he was being framed by the FBI. But the House Un-American Activities Committee (HUAC) started a highly publicized investigation (led by Congressman Richard M. Nixon, who made a name for himself by going after Hiss) that quickly brought the alleged spy to trial. Because Hiss

(Right) Alger Hiss was accused of selling secrets to the Russians in the 1940s and given a five-year sentence for perjury in 1950. His much publicized trial, initiated by the House Un-American Activities Committee, made many Americans wonder how many other Communist traitors were waiting to come out of the woodwork.

was charged more than seven years after he allegedly committed the crime, he could no longer be tried for treason, but only for perjury. On January 21, 1950, he was found guilty and given a five-year sentence.

Although he was convicted of perjury and not of treason, Americans were shocked and stunned. Many were convinced that he was, in fact, a traitor. In their eyes, the State Department, the United Nations (which Hiss had backed), Democratic liberals, and the entire Truman administration came under suspicion just by their previous association with Hiss. Even more frightening was the question: How many more Alger Hisses were still operating in America?

The Press and the Public Image

The press took these fears and ran with them. Major magazines started running feature articles with titles such as "Communists Penetrate Wall Street," "Russian Spies: Trained to Raise Hell in America," "Reds Are After Your Child," and "How Communists Take Over." One supposedly true story of a Communist who turned FBI informer ("I Led Three Lives" by Herbert Philbrick) was serialized in more than five hundred newspapers across the country. Anti-Communist, anti-Soviet books became instant bestsellers. Even Hollywood got on the bandwagon, producing such box-office thrillers as *I Married a Communist*, *The Red Menace*, *Guilty of Treason*, and *I Was a Communist for the FBI*.

The public ate it up, and the Communist image took on grotesque proportions. Communists were depicted as devious and highly skilled fiends who could hypnotize ordinary citizens into succumbing to their evil doctrines. American fear and hatred of Communists escalated to such a feverish pitch that it became acceptable for people to heckle and persecute anyone they suspected of being a Communist sympathizer. In this growing hysteria, members of the country's Socialist party were often falsely labeled Communists by the press and were shouted at, tormented, and stoned when they attempted to hold any political or social functions. In fact, anyone who did not fit the status quo image of white, middle-class, Protestant America became potential Communist sympathizers in many people's eyes. That category included African-Americans, Asian-Americans, Jews, union organizers, immigrants, liberal college professors, and many others.

It's no wonder that one of the most popular fictional characters in the early 1950s was Mickey Spillane's gutsy American hero, Mike Hammer. In *One Lonely Night*, Hammer brags "I killed more people tonight than I have fingers on my hands. I shot them in cold blood and enjoyed every minute of it. I shot slugs into the nastiest bunch of bastards you ever saw. They were Commies. They were red sons-of-bitches who should have died long ago. They never thought there were people like me in this country. They figured us all to be as soft as horse manure and just as stupid."

The Cold War and a Real One

Although the two superpowers, the U.S. and the USSR, waged a tense Cold War and were busy stockpiling

U.S. Marines were ill-equipped for the bitter winter conditions in Korea and suffered demoralizing losses at the hands of the North Korean and Chinese soldiers, who unexpectedly carried out a series of frontal attacks on American positions near the Chinese-Korean border in December 1950.

enough nuclear weapons to blow up every person on earth several times over, the nuclear war everyone dreaded never came to pass. Instead, tension built throughout the fifties through many smaller crises as the so-called forces of democracy fought the spread of communism in remote corners of the earth. The first and bloodiest of these confrontations was in a tiny Asian country called Korea.

The same year that Alger Hiss was sentenced, just five years after the end of World War II, U.S. soldiers found themselves fighting another bitter war in a tiny country of rice paddies, rolling hills, and rugged mountains. Korea had often been a battleground between China, Japan, and Russia, but it was not a particularly strategic area for the United States. In fact, most Americans had never heard of it before. It was not a particularly pleasant place to fight a war, either, with its harsh terrain and a climate of extremes, ranging from 105 degrees in the summer to 40 degrees below zero in the winter.

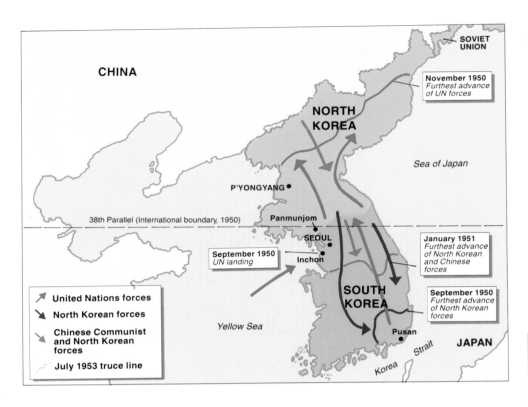

This map shows the major movements of UN and North Korean forces during the Korean War of 1950-1953.

Map labels:

CHINA

SOVIET UNION

NORTH KOREA

November 1950
Furthest advance of UN forces

Sea of Japan

P'YONGYANG

38th Parallel (International boundary, 1950)

Panmunjom

SEOUL

September 1950
UN landing

Inchon

January 1951
Furthest advance of North Korean and Chinese forces

September 1950
Furthest advance of North Korean forces

SOUTH KOREA

Yellow Sea

Pusan

JAPAN

Korea Strait

↗ United Nations forces

↘ North Korean forces

↘ Chinese Communist and North Korean forces

⤴ July 1953 truce line

By the time of this "peace action," Korea had already been war ravaged for more than fifty years. Japan had controlled Korea since defeating Russia in 1905 and ruled it brutally until the end of World War II, when the country was liberated by the Allied powers. Like much of Europe after that war, Korea was temporarily divided, with the northern half occupied by Soviet troops and the southern half occupied by the United States. The dividing line was the thirty-eighth parallel, the latitude line that divided the country into two almost equal north and south sections. The People's Democratic Republic of North Korea was led by Kim Il Sung, a veteran Communist, and the Republic of South Korea was headed by a Korean nationalist named Syngman Rhee. Both Kim and Rhee were itching to take over the other's country and claim all of Korea for their own.

As agreed in the peace talks following World War II, the Soviets ended their occupation of northern Korea in 1949, but they left behind a well-trained North Korean army backed by Soviet tanks and planes. The United States also withdrew its troops from the south in 1949, but because they were afraid that Rhee would use them to overrun North Korea, they deliberately did not supply the ragtag South Korean army with heavy weapons.

On June 25, 1950, Kim Il Sung, who had deliberately waited until the start of Korea's summer monsoons, led his North Korean troops across the thirty-eighth parallel in a surprise invasion of South Korea. The United Nations, which believed the Soviets had put the North Koreans up to the attack, immediately passed several resolutions condemning the North Koreans for their aggression and

"The attack upon Korea makes it plain that Communism has passed beyond the use of subversion to conquer independent nations and will now use armed invasion and war. Accordingly, I have ordered the Seventh Fleet to prevent any attack on Formosa."

Harry S Truman, 1950

United Nations forces, headed by American troops in Patton tanks, were originally sent into Korea to defend their South Korean ally against Communist troops. By the fall of 1950, following MacArthur's successful offensive at Inchon, that strategy had changed to a plan to conquor North Korea and unify the two Koreas under a pro-western government.

ªauthorized America to lead UN troops to defend South Korea. The Soviet Union, a member of the UN Security Council, could have vetoed the Korean resolution, but was boy-cotting the UN at the time for its refusal to allow Communist China to join.

President Truman also responded immediately. Without waiting for approval from Congress, he ordered support troops be sent to South Korea and named the respected World War II hero General Douglas MacArthur as UN troop commander.

Truman called it a "United Nations police action" instead of what it really was: a war between the U.S. and North Korea. Although sixteen nations contributed soldiers, most of

the fighting troops were American and General MacArthur took his orders directly from Truman, rather than from the United Nations. In spite of the president's careful description, it was an American war.

An Unpopular War

From the beginning, it was a very unpopular war for most Americans. Although many people owned televi-sion sets by 1950, TV journalists did not yet have the technology to present the Korean War to the American pub-lic live and in color on television, as they did for the Vietnam War a few years later. For the most part, the best reporting was done by print journalists

who tried to capture the suffering and heroism of American soldiers. But they were doing so for a public who for the most part didn't care, who couldn't even pronounce the names of the places where the troops were fighting and who did not want to hear such grim news anyway. They had enough to worry about with the hydrogen bomb and Communists supposedly infiltrating the PTA. Unlike World War II, which had captured the enthusiasm and support of the entire nation, the Korean war was one Americans barely tolerated. Once it was over, they could not wait to forget it: It was not the subject of movies, plays, and novels, and returning veterans were not given the heroes' welcome veterans had received after World War II.

The first six weeks of the war were disastrous for U.S. and South Korean troops. The better-trained and better-equipped North Korean forces had pushed them all the way back to the tip of the peninsula. General MacArthur then launched his brilliant counterattack. By surprising the North Koreans with an amphibious attack on the city of Inchon at the same time his ground forces were striking at the city of Pusan, MacArthur's UN troops were able to achieve their objective, driving the North Korean troops back across the thirty-eighth parallel. MacArthur's strategy was considered a stroke of genius, but it was also his last real victory. He thought he saw an opportunity to become even more of a hero by going a step further and taking over North Korea. It was a fatal mistake.

Truman was afraid that MacArthur would provoke Chinese leader Mao Zedong into sending his Communist troops in to defend North Korea, which would put the U.S. at war with China. MacArthur assured him that the Chinese talked a good game but that they would never send troops into North Korea to fight the United States. Even if they did, MacArthur said, they would be no match for the UN troops. He

As battle-ready American troops push north over miles of difficult terrain in their efforts to overrun the Communists, South Korean women and children flee south in terror from the North Korean invaders.

promised Truman he was already on the brink of victory and that he'd have the boys home by Christmas.

MacArthur, however, was so cocky about his upcoming victory that he failed to gather intelligence reports about what was happening on the

The Korean War, fought so soon after the end of World War II, took a further heavy toll of dead and wounded.

U.S. CASUALTIES IN THE KOREAN WAR / June 25, 1950 TO July 27, 1953

	NUMBER IN SERVICE	WOUNDED	DIED IN BATTLE	OTHER DEATHS	TOTAL DEAD
ARMY	2,834,000	77,596	27,704	9,429	37,133
NAVY	1,177,000	1,576	458	4,043	4,501
MARINES	424,000	23,744	4,267	1,261	5,528
AIR FORCE	1,285,000	368	1,200	5,884	7,084
TOTAL	5,720,000	103,284	33,629	20,617	54,246

"If you can't stand the heat, get out of the kitchen.

Harry S Truman

Chinese-Korean border. He also failed to take the time to learn anything about Mao's new highly trained army. MacArthur sent his troops even deeper into North Korea without realizing that they had neither the weapons nor the clothing to withstand the bitter cold temperatures of up to thirty below zero. When they approached the Chinese-Korean border, they were smashed by a million well-armed and warmly dressed Chinese who had crossed the border undetected by American intelligence.

The war quickly became a nightmare for the United States forces during the winter of 1950-1951. Back home, Americans now felt angry and humiliated because U.S. troops had been forced to retreat by the Communist Chinese. People were calling it "Truman's War," "the no-win war," and "the Democrats' war." Even through MacArthur was a beloved American hero, when he publicly denounced the Truman administration for refusing to bomb and invade China to win the war, Truman fired him —amidst a huge public outcry — and replaced him with General Matthew Ridgway. Only then did the badly demoralized UN troops have a chance to regroup against the Chinese and North Koreans.

Finally, a Cease-Fire

On June 23, 1951, the Russian ambassador to the United Nations proposed a cease-fire to allow armistice talks, but it took another two years to negotiate boundary lines and exchange prisoners of war. Unfortunately, while the diplomats negotiated, the fighting went on, and thousands of men continued to die. The war did not end, in fact, until the summer of 1953. By that time, 54,246 Americans had died, and another 103,000 had been wounded.

Back home, many Americans believed the war had dragged on because the Truman administration was soft on communism, and in 1952, their votes reflected their anger. When the smoke had cleared and the votes were counted, the Democrats were out and the Republicans were in, both in Congress and the White House.

After five months of negotiations, the Korean military armistice was signed in November, 1951. Here, Communist representatives sign the agreement of the neutral zone. But the cease-fire did not hold, and fighting continued until the middle of 1953.

Eisenhower, the World War II hero, had been elected president.

The Effects of the Korean War

The Korean War had a mixed effect on the American economy, leading to inflation, industrial shortages, and wage and price controls. More Americans than ever before were employed and had money to spend on consumer goods that could raise their standard of living. As a result, the demand for everything from nylon stockings to TV sets and cars was at an all-time high. Yet the Korean War was still the nation's first priority, which meant industry had to focus on arms production and troop support. One significant impact was the profitable defense contracts it brought to manufacturers — contracts to build B-52 bombers, a nuclear navy, guided missiles, and, of course, hydrogen bombs. After the Korean War, Congress authorized even more defense spending, which made weapons manufacturing a very profitable business in the 1950s.

A major positive effect of the war was the racial integration of the U.S. Army and the Marine Corps. Lt. Col. Frank L. Petersen became the highest ranking African-American officer in the marines and the first black marine flyer in war, where he distinguished himself flying sixty-four successful combat missions. This integration and belated recognition of heroic African- and Hispanic-Americans, and American Indians was a small first step in a battle for racial equality that did not reach full momentum until the 1960s.

Meanwhile, More Spies

While United Nations troops were fighting the Communists in Korea, anticommunist sentiment con-

"All my life I have fought against prejudice and intolerance."

Harry S Truman

tinued to gather force back home. Early in 1950, Dr. Klaus Fuchs, a British scientist who had worked on the U.S. atom bomb project, was tried on charges of supplying atom bomb secrets to the Soviets. During his trial, he admitted giving them this information between 1942 and 1947, and he was convicted and sentenced to four-

Lt. Col. Frank L. Petersen, first African-American flyer in the Korean war and a distinguished marine, represented long-awaited recognition for black officers in the U.S. armed forces.

teen years in prison. His trial immediately triggered an investigation of his potential accomplices and led to the arrest of Harry Gold (a Philadelphia chemist), David Greenglass (a machinist who had worked at the atom bomb research facility), Greenglass's wife, Ruth, and his sister and brother-in-law, Ethel and Julius Rosenberg. Sev-

eral acquaintances of the Rosenbergs were also arrested.

The breaking of this ring of spies caused a tremendous sensation in the American press. Because all the defendants happened to be Jewish, many people immediately jumped to the conclusion that there was an international Jewish conspiracy behind the spread of communism and, in fact, behind all of the problems plaguing the U.S. and the rest of the free world.

Millions began to believe that all of the country's troubles were caused by a growing and poisonous Communist conspiracy, a conspiracy that was not fomenting across the ocean somewhere but right in their own back yards. It was in this atmosphere of the Red Scare that Wisconsin Senator Joseph McCarthy rose to power.

The Rise and Fall of Joe McCarthy

Less than a week after the Fuchs story broke in the press, Senator McCarthy began his anticommunist witch hunt. Addressing a chapter of the Republican Women's Club in Wheeling, West Virginia, in February, 1950, he waved a piece of paper and claimed that he had a list of 205 State Department officials who were known to be members of the Communist party. (What he actually waved was his own laundry list, but no one else knew that.) The following night, McCarthy gave the same speech in Salt Lake City and then several days later in Reno, Nevada, though the number of Communist infiltrators kept changing with each speech. It didn't take long before this senator had the whole nation's attention. His next step was to take his charges to the

Ethel Rosenberg. (1916-1953)

Were Julius and Ethel Rosenberg vicious spies who sold out their country? Or were they innocent victims of anticommunist hysteria? No one to this day knows whether the couple deserved to die as they did, in the electric chair. . . .

Ethel was born and reared on the Lower East Side of New York City. She wanted to go to college, but there was no money when she graduated from high school during the Great Depression in 1931. Instead, she took a stenographic course, found a job, and devoted much of her time to amateur theatrical productions. Possessed of a good voice, she became the youngest member of a respected professional choir.

The young woman also showed an interest in left-wing politics, supporting several labor union causes and suing successfully after being fired from her job because of her union activities. In 1936, at a fundraising affair, she met her future husband, Julius. Three years younger than Ethel and a college student, he was persuaded by her to finish school rather than dropping out to pursue a life of radical political organizing. Nevertheless, Julius joined the Communist party in 1936, three years before the couple married.

The Rosenbergs settled into married life, he as an engineer with the United States Signal Corps, she as a typist for the U.S. Bureau of the Census and then as a new mother. They lived modestly in a low-cost New York City public housing project, keeping to themselves and doting on their two sons. Julius was fired from the Signal Corps in 1945 for past political activity and later attempted to start a machine shop with David Greenglass, Ethel's brother. The business venture was a flop.

In 1950, a chemist caught spying for the Soviet Union claimed to have passed atomic secrets to David Greenglass. Greenglass told authorities he had been recruited by Julius Rosenberg. Julius was arrested and imprisoned. Ethel was called before a grand jury, arrested, and held illegally for eight months without being charged with a crime. Ruth Greenglass, David's wife, claimed that Ethel typed the information brought to her husband by David. Ethel and Julius steadfastly denied involvement in any kind of spy ring.

The government's case against Ethel was especially weak, in part because not one typed note was ever found. However, circumstances were stacked against her. First, she was an admitted leftist, which was itself considered subversive in the 1950s. Second, the authorities wanted to use her to force Julius to admit wrongdoing. And third, Judge Irving Kaufman, a Jew, did not want to appear to be soft on two fellow Jews accused of selling out their country. The Rosenbergs were tried, convicted, and sentenced to death in 1951.

The couple communicated from their prison cells mostly by writing. Ethel's letters were heartfelt and wrenching, particularly those written to her two young sons. She reminded them of their parents' innocence, stating that it would "wrong our conscience" to admit to something neither had done. The letters were made public to raise funds for an appeal, which was finally turned down by President Eisenhower. The two died in the Sing Sing prison electric chair in upstate New York on June 19, 1953.

The Army-McCarthy hearings of 1954. After the televised hearings, which were viewed by an estimated twenty million Americans, McCarthy was censured by the Senate for engaging in conduct "unbecoming a member of the United States Senate."

Senate, where he held the floor for six straight hours, raging out his accusations and demanding that the Senate indict the people on his list.

Congress had already been concerned enough about potential Communist infiltrators to pass an anti-communist bill in 1950, the McCarran Internal Security Act, over President Truman's veto, who thought the act unconstitutional. So when they heard McCarthy's accusations, Congress took them seriously and it responded by establishing a special Senate investigative committee. For several months, this committee tracked down every one of McCarthy's leads, sorted through all of the evidence, and carefully listened to all the testimony.

In June, they made their report:

Not one of McCarthy's accusations turned out to be true. All of his cases had been based on rumor, gossip, and lies. The committee even went so far as to label McCarthy's charges a fraud and a hoax. But instead of putting Senator McCarthy in his place, the committee's report had exactly the opposite effect. Many people (especially Republicans) were disgusted with the committee's report, claiming that it was just another government attempt to protect Communist traitors. Instead of losing power, McCarthy became stronger and even more feared. Two years later, when Republican candidate Dwight Eisenhower was elected president and the Republicans gained control of Congress, they immediately rewarded

Senator McCarthy with the chairmanship of his own permanent investigating subcommittee.

McCarthy quickly became a popular American hero. To his followers, he was "Tail Gunner Joe," the all-American war hero they could trust to root out the traitors and who would make sure they got what they deserved. He had the backing of many mainstream institutions, from the American Legion and Veterans of Foreign Wars to national Catholic and Protestant organizations who saw in him a protector against the spread of Communist atheism.

The fact that McCarthy was never able to prove any of his charges got very little attention from the press, while his accusations always made front-page headlines. With few exceptions, even journalists were pro-McCarthy for the five years he remained in power. During those five years, his vicious slander and outrageous charges ruined the lives of thousands of innocent people, including writers, actors, and producers in the entertainment industry. (McCarthy seemed to have a personal vendetta against Hollywood.) Over six hundred college professors were fired. Many public libraries were forced to remove books by Communist, Socialist, liberal, and even black authors. Politicians on every level of government were scrutinized.

McCarthy's downfall finally began when he took on the U.S. Army. In the summer of 1954, the Senate started a thirty-five day investigation into army allegations that McCarthy tried to get preferential treatment (on more than ninety separate occasions) for his young assistant, Private G. David Schine. These hearings were televised nationally and gave millions of Americans the opportunity to see for themselves how this Communist witch hunter worked as he attacked and slandered the army's respected top brass. His popularity declined sharply. Before the army hearings were over, the Senate started an investigation of its own into McCarthy's conduct as a senator, an investigation that resulted in an official Senate censure, or condemnation, of his previous conduct. Although he remained a senator, McCarthy was a broken man after this censure.

Witch Hunt Waxes and Wanes

Horrific as his reign of terror was, it is important to note that McCarthy did not start the Red Scare, but merely capitalized on it. He was not the only one hunting Communists, and the end of McCarthy was by no means the end of the witch hunt. The House Un-American Activities Committee (HUAC), which was already in action years before McCarthy rose to power, continued its hunt for reds throughout the fifties, although it did so without as much of the previous publicity.

Other government agencies were also actively involved in this pursuit, such as the Internal Security Committee, the FBI, and the CIA. J. Edgar Hoover, head of the Federal Bureau of Investigation for twenty-five years, started his own hunt for reds as soon as World War II ended. Believing that a third of the world's population was in on this great Communist conspiracy, Hoover had FBI agents, telephone tappers, handwriting experts, informants, and spies working full time investigating and compiling files on

> *"[The U.S. needs a] deterrent of massive retaliatory power. . . a great capacity to retaliate instantly by means and at times of our own choosing."*
>
> Secretary of State, John Foster Dulles, 1954

> *"Nothing is easy in war. Mistakes are always paid for in casualties and troops are quick to sense any blunder made by their commanders."*
>
> Dwight D. Eisenhower, 1953

John Foster Dulles. (1888-1959)

John Foster Dulles' humorless preoccupation with communism was to influence the United States for many years following World War II.

A lawyer by trade, Dulles represented his country at the post-World War I Paris Peace Conference in 1919, took part in drafting the preamble to the United Nations Charter in 1945, and served for three years as America's UN delegate. Dwight Eisenhower, elected president in 1952, named Dulles as his secretary of state. The secretary immediately refuted Harry Truman's plan to contain Soviet communism, preferring instead to attempt to roll back the frontiers of Communist influence.

Dulles, a deeply religious man who was convinced that lying was the consistent policy of the Soviet Union, preferred not to tip his rivals by threatening them. Instead, he wanted to practice "brinksmanship," whereby the Communists were forced to back down on any given point by the threat of massive retaliation from the United States and its allies. He refused to believe that the rift between the Soviet Union and China was real, and he did not care if a country was democratic, so long as it was noncommunist.

The secretary, who died in office, was almost as scornful of British and European colonial rule. He felt that the United States was an anticolonial beacon to Africans, Asians, and South Americans. He believed that, once freed, the colonies would be attracted to western democracy and repelled by communism, making them automatic American allies. Appeasement was not in his vocabulary. Dulles' hatred of the Soviet Union enlarged the fears of earlier Democrats and Republicans alike and led to years of brushfire wars and wasteful military spending.

millions of suspected American citizens. Even after the Army-McCarthy hearings exposed Senator McCarthy for what he was, a Gallup Poll revealed that at least 36 percent of the people in America still supported what he had done.

By 1953, however, most of the American public was tired of the feverish anticommunist hysteria and wanted a rest. They had elected Eisenhower, a safe, fatherly general, to preside in the White House and keep them safe. The economy was booming, and Americans wanted to forget their fears and enjoy their newfound prosperity. In some respects the Eisenhower era allowed them to do that. But the fifties also had their share of international crises.

Eisenhower and the Cold War

Dwight D. Eisenhower, victorious commander of the Allied troops in Europe in World War II, was the well-liked war hero the Republicans talked into running for president in 1952. "Ike," as he was affectionately known, was elected by a landslide, but he won on more than just his wartime reputation. His fatherly presence seemed to assure Americans that everything was going to be okay, that they were good people who deserved to enjoy prosperity and freedom from nuclear attack.

Ending the Korean War was not Eisenhower's only Cold War crisis, however. He confronted Communists in Europe, Africa, Asia, and South America, even on the island of Cuba, just ninety miles off the Florida coast. He also had to deal with the U.S.-Soviet space race (as discussed in the next chapter), the nuclear arms race, and the nasty business of international spies.

Just before Eisenhower was reelected to a second term in 1956, fighting broke out in Egypt when that nation's leader, Gamal Abdel Nasser, nationalized the British-controlled Suez Canal. In late October of 1956, British, French, and Israeli forces had invaded Egypt to regain the Suez canal and called on the United States for support. This put President Eisenhower on the spot. The Soviet Union was threatening to intervene, and Nasser also had the support of various discontented African nations. This convinced Eisenhower that the Egyptian invasion had to be stopped, and he pressured Britain, France, and Israel, who had already regained control of the Suez canal, to withdraw and agree to a cease-fire. Although a major war was averted, the countries involved in the abortive invasion came to resent the United States for not backing them against Egypt, and the western anti-Soviet alliance was considerably weakened.

That same month, the Soviet Union invaded Hungary to crush an anticommunist uprising. For several years after the death of Soviet dictator Stalin in 1953, people living in some of the satellite countries of the Soviet Union demonstrated for reforms. On October 23, 1956, violence erupted in Budapest, when police fired upon a crowd of students who were demonstrating peacefully. Fighting broke out all over Hungary, encouraged by Radio Free Europe, a broadcasting program of the United States that implied help was on the way. But the Soviets, who knew the world was preoccupied with the Suez crisis and who were assured by President Eisenhower that the U.S. would not intervene, brutally and quickly crushed the revolution. Within a few weeks, Hungary was in shambles, tens of thousands of people had been killed or imprisoned, and over two hundred thousand more were forced to flee the country. People throughout the world, especially Americans, were outraged.

But perhaps even more than that, they were scared. For a few weeks, tensions were so great over what the Soviets had done that the world seemed on the brink of nuclear war. More than ever, Americans became preoccupied with bomb shelters and civil defense procedures, anything that could help them survive the horrors of the nuclear war they were convinced the Soviets would eventually provoke.

"[The U.S. and the USSR] are like two scorpions in a bottle, each capable of killing each other but only at the risk of his own life. . . .The atomic clock ticks faster and faster."

J. Robert Oppenheimer, atomic scientist, 1956

The bullet-sprayed window of Port Said's lighthouse looks out on the Norwegian tanker Eli Knudson, sailing out of the Suez Canal in January 1957. It had been trapped there for two months during the Suez Crisis in the fall of 1956, when British, French, and Israeli forces invaded Egypt in an attempt to regain control of the canal.

Communist Confrontations

In its attempts to contain the spread of communism, the U.S. even had its hand in African politics. Due largely to the efforts of the Pan-African League, a newly formed organization of prominent black political leaders, seventeen separate African nations demanded and won independence from their European colonial rulers in 1957. The Pan-African

League also had the support of many African-American leaders, who were also fighting for desegregation and equal rights within the United States. Other Americans had a different reason to be interested in African politics —fear of the spread of communism. Bloody power struggles often ensued within these African countries after they gained independence, and the Soviets aided the procommunist forces in hopes of setting up a procommunist regime. The United States, paranoid about the potential spread of communism, felt obliged to support the prowestern factions.

A particularly tense confrontation took place in what was formerly the Belgian Congo. After the native nationalists forced out the Belgians, they renamed their country Zaire. Many Americans believed that when Patrice Lumumba, one of the nationalist revolutionaries who had definite Communist leanings, succeeded in seizing power, Zaire would soon become a puppet government of the Soviets. To prevent this from happening, Eisenhower supposedly ordered the CIA to "eliminate" Lumumba. The CIA agents did their best (with a number of schemes involving exotic poisons and other sophisticated assassination attempts), but when all of their attempts failed, the U.S. was forced to try another approach. They made sure that Lumumba's rival, General Joseph Mobutu, gained enough power to overthrow him; he subsequently had Lumumba killed.

Two of the leaders of the Hungarian uprising against Soviet domination stand holding the Hungarian Nationalist flag in Budapest, in November 1956. Confident that the rest of the world was busy with the Suez crisis, the Soviet Union quickly subdued the revolution. Eyewitnesses reported that freedom fighters were hanged from bridges over the Danube or were shot on sight.

Fidel Castro was one Communist threat that the CIA could not eliminate, despite numerous assassination attempts. Castro's successful revolt against Cuban dictator Fulgencio Batista in 1959 set up a dictatorship in America's back yard. Communist Cuba has remained a thorn in the American side ever since.

Other Communist confrontations Eisenhower had to deal with hit painfully close to home. Communist leader Fidel Castro Ruz led a revolt against Cuban dictator Fulgencio Batista in 1959 and has ruled Cuba ever since. At first, he had the support of the Cuban people because he worked hard to improve the living conditions of the poor. But when he started to confiscate property owned by foreigners and began killing or deporting anyone who disagreed with him, thousands of middle-class and

professional Cubans realized he was setting up a Communist dictatorship and left the island. Many emigrated to the United States, settling primarily in Miami and other large cities along the East Coast, where they faced much resentment and discrimination.

The U–2 Affair

In May 1960, two weeks before President Eisenhower was scheduled to meet with Soviet premier Nikita Khrushchev at an important summit conference, the Soviets announced that an American flyer, Francis Gary Powers, had been shot down in a U-2 spy plane over Soviet territory. The summit conference was immediately cancelled. At first, American officials, assuming that their CIA pilot would take his suicide pill and not expose them, claimed that the U-2 was a weather plane that had strayed off course over Russian territory by accident. But then Powers himself confessed to being a spy and was sentenced to ten years in a Soviet prison (of which he eventually only served two years).

A very embarrassed U.S. State Department then admitted that the U-2 had been engaged in espionage activities, but claimed that these activities had not been authorized by the government. Later that month, President Eisenhower himself changed that position and admitted that Powers' spying had been fully approved and authorized by the U.S. government. The president refused to apologize to the Soviet government, though, arguing that the Soviets had known about the spy missions for years and had never complained about them before.

The most important effect of the incident was that it caused the media to step back and question America's goals and ideology for the first time. Mass magazines such as *Look,* and *Life,* and the *New York Times* featured a number of articles discussing the United States' national intentions and future role in international politics. Many of these articles criticized American values for being too materialistic and consumer-oriented, and began to focus on the realities of poverty and social inequality, setting the stage for the social revolution that would erupt in the 1960s.

American U-2 spy pilot Francis Gary Powers stands in a Soviet court after being found guilty of espionage and sentenced to ten years' imprisonment. Powers' capture by the Soviet Union and his subsequent confession wrecked imminent summit talks between Eisenhower and Soviet premier Khrushchev.

CHAPTER 7
About the Bomb

The twenty-five crew members of the Japanese fishing vessel *Lucky Dragon* may not have noticed the absence of other ships in the Pacific on the fateful day of March 1, 1954. Without warning, their predawn sky was bathed in a brilliant light, followed by a shock wave and a huge, horizontal cloud — the fishing boat had sailed too near one of the first U.S. hydrogen bomb tests. This explosion, on a tiny hunk of coral called the Bikini Atoll, caused all on board to suffer radiation sickness from the effects of

The New York Journal American *published this dummy front page on behalf of the Office of Civil Defense, which distributed it in the area affected by the "raid" as a taste of what might be yet to come.*

"The Soviet government deems it necessary to report that the United States has no monopoly in the production of the hydrogen bomb."

Soviet premier Georgi Malenkov, 1953

the fallout. One crew member died before the year was out. Unfortunately, the *Lucky Dragon* crewmen weren't the only people too near the blast.

More than seven thousand square miles of ocean became contaminated, as did 239 residents of the Marshall Islands and twenty-eight American service personnel. What awesome power had caused such widespread damage? The hydrogen bomb, first tested by the United States in 1952 and by the Soviet Union a year later, was one hundred times more destructive than either of the two bombs dropped on the Japanese in 1945 to help end World War II. The very existence of nuclear weapons as devastating as these changed the way Americans felt about the past, the present, and the future.

Before the invention of atomic weapons, Americans believed they had some control over their lives. Wars happened elsewhere, economic recessions eventually ended, droughts didn't last forever — but a bomb capable of killing millions, dropped without warning, was something that could not be anticipated, but only feared. Fear became almost visible, as the Soviet Union produced atomic weapons that apparently matched those manufactured for possible use by U.S. armed forces.

Negative Views

By the time of the first hydrogen bomb test, most Americans had strong opinions about war, atomic weapons, and the Soviet Union. They felt that differences between Americans and Soviets would never be reconciled; they were convinced that Soviet communism could not be changed; they believed that nuclear weaponry, once invented, would never go away, so that the threat of nuclear war should be the basis for national security; and they feared that the Soviet Union, with less to lose, would surprise the U.S. in a sneak attack and, after wiping out North America, would quickly rule the world.

The most obvious result of this grim outlook was the Cold War. From 1945 until 1990, the United States and the Soviet Union threatened each other with nuclear destruction. To be precise, each believed in mutually assured destruction, aptly shortened to MAD. Mutually assured destruction

Graphic illustrations like this montage of an atomic bomb exploding over New York City and the fake news report on the facing page did nothing to defuse Americans' fear of nuclear war.

> *"On watch 24 hours a day, DEW [that's Distant Early Warning] will probe the polar sky with radar. The DEW line will stand between you and a sneak attack over the top of the world."*
>
> Douglas Aircraft ad, 1956

A network of radar stations like this one, 110 miles east of Cape Cod, Massachusetts, were intended to detect enemy planes or missiles before they reached the United States and were used to reassure Americans nervous about the risks of nuclear attack by the Soviet Union.

meant that either side had enough weaponry to wipe out the other, no matter who began the war or how many bombs were dropped by the one who started it. The two superpowers battled for the hearts and minds of Europeans, Africans, Asians, and South Americans by handing out money, food, and conventional weapons. The implied threat of atomic weaponry was present wherever the two tangled. As the decade proceeded, Soviet and U.S. military bases bristled with weapons, some of them nuclear and ready for use.

A Gallup Poll taken in 1950 indicated that 70 percent of those surveyed believed the Soviet Union wanted to rule the world. Some 41 percent of these citizens felt that the U.S. would fight another war (besides Korea) within five years. Three-quarters of those questioned said they feared that American cities would be bombed in the next war. Finally, 19 percent believed that the next world war, when it came, would wipe out the human race. Anyone who recalls the 1950s as a light-hearted time should be reminded of the weighty burden of the threat of nuclear war and of communism on the minds of the American public.

A Secret Document on America's Defense

The Truman administration knew very well how Americans felt and it acted accordingly. In 1950, the National Security Council (the president's most trusted defense advisors) issued a secret document that would become the blueprint for U.S. conduct for the next twenty years. Rabidly anticommunist and militaristic, the memorandum known as NSC-68 was conceived to maintain a balance of power between America and the Soviet Union. In addition to backing the buildup of superior nuclear and conventional arms, the memo spoke out against attempting to negotiate with the enemy. The motivation for NSC-68 was the government's belief that the Soviets were bent on world conquest. No wonder average Americans were similarly paranoid — though some of the warlike words were aimed at silencing Republicans and conservatives who felt the Democrats were soft on communism.

NSC-68 wasn't the only path to survival. In 1952, the U.S. contracted with Western Electric to build the Distant Early Warning, or DEW, line across the top of Canada. This network of radar stations scanned the skies in order to pick up Soviet planes or missiles traveling across the North Pole to attack North America. The DEW line was one of three such installations. Hundreds of miles south was a similar system, called the Mid-Canada Line, that stretched from the southern tip of Alaska to Labrador. And along the American-Canadian border was the Pine Tree Line. Soviet aircraft frequently tested U.S. radar by flying into areas being scanned, and

U.S. planes based in places such as Turkey and Iran did the same thing to check out the potential enemy.

The first line of America's defense became the U.S. Air Force Strategic Air Command (SAC). The force was made up of huge bombers, each with a dozen crew members. Based primarily within the continental United States, a number of the aircraft were kept in the air at all times to retaliate if America came under attack by dropping nuclear weapons on the Soviets. One of the decade's most common pieces of aerial film footage showed a massive SAC bomber being refueled via a long hose in midair so that the plane could bomb Moscow, Leningrad, or Stalingrad and, presumably, make it back to the U.S.

The cost of maintaining SAC forces — of building bombs and missiles, constructing missile silos, building radar sites, and providing soldiers and supplies for bases worldwide — was staggering. One example of the money needed to keep SAC bombers ready for war involved the purchase of hundreds of big, four-wheel-drive trucks. Equipped with snowplows, the trucks roared in formation down runways at bases in places like North Dakota and the upper peninsula of Michigan, pushing heavy snow aside. The trucks were used less than half the year and served no other function. No one asked how the enemy kept its snowy runways clear, but there was the suspicion that the USSR relied instead on an army of workers wielding brooms!

Because of the grim nature of the arms race, nothing gave Americans much comfort. When Soviet dictator Josef Stalin died of a brain hemorrhage in 1953, the immediate fear among government experts was that someone even worse would take his place. Stalin had orchestrated the domination of eastern Europe by Communist puppet governments and had given aid and comfort to Chinese Communists in their successful drive to take over their country. Immediately after his death, presidential advisors longed to deal with Stalin because they felt they understood him. He seemed more reluctant than most Soviets to start World War III.

The Soviet *Sputnik*

October 4, 1957, was a pleasant fall day in the nation's capital, and President Dwight D. Eisenhower told his staff he intended to play golf tomorrow. The golf outing took place, even though Americans were learning to their exasperation that the Soviet Union had successfully launched into orbit a 184-pound sphere that carried a radio transmitter. The device included enough batteries to make it beep for two weeks and

Mounted on its stand at a secret launch site, the Russian space satellite Sputnik *is shown here shortly before its launch into space in October 1957. Terrified that the Soviets could now fire nuclear missiles at the United States, and desperate to keep up in the space race, the United States launched their Navy Vanguard rocket bearing a grapefruit-sized satellite shortly afterward. It rose a few feet off the launch pad before collapsing in flames.*

Wernher von Braun. (1912-1977)

Before *Sputnik,* few Americans had heard of Wernher von Braun. The German rocket scientist had, as a young man, played an important role in the design and construction of V-2 rockets. These powerful weapons were used against Britain in World War II in an attempt by Hitler to reverse Germany's defeat. Shortly after Hitler's death in 1945, von Braun and other important rocket scientists surrendered to U.S. forces and wound up American citizens.

Work began on a rather low-key space program as early as 1949. Meetings were devoted to the problem of weightlessness and other challenges. Huntsville, Alabama, became a center for rocket research and experimentation, and von Braun was closely involved in such activities. He spent much of his time stumping for additional money so that the U.S. could beat the Soviets into the heavens.

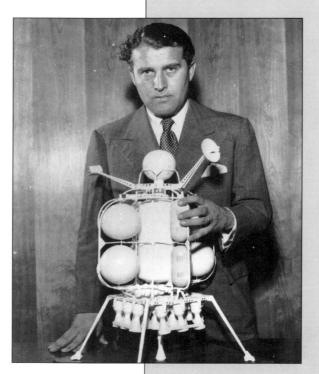

This country's scientists were shocked when the Soviet Union fired the first artificial object into space in 1957. Shortly after *Sputnik's* triumph, a U.S. Navy rocket with a five-pound instrument package was launched into the heavens. It traveled a few feet before collapsing in flames. Von Braun and his peers were called in and quickly launched *Explorer I* in 1958. It was the first U.S. earth satellite to go into orbit, and it established Cape Canaveral as the primary launching pad into space, also discovering the Van Allen radiation belt encircling the earth.

Nevertheless, the U.S. played catch-up for several years with the Soviet Union. Von Braun helped the country break even with the Soviets and then pull ahead by working on a series of Saturn rockets for the Apollo lunar missions in the late 1960s. Even before the first person was shot into space, though, scientists knew it could be done. Their fear was that, once in space, the astronaut could not be retrieved alive. Much of the latter part of the 1950s was spent plotting a successful round trip, which occurred with Alan B. Shepard, Jr., in 1961.

Von Braun continued to play a key role in the American-Soviet space race, including the triumphant landing on the moon in 1969. He died of natural causes in 1977.

> *"[Sputnik] is a hunk of iron anybody could launch."*
>
> Rear admiral
> Lawson Bennett, 1957

featured four swept-back antennas. United States scientists from the Arctic Circle to the middle of the Pacific Ocean could pick up the first artificial satellite's signal as it circled the earth. Though it carried no scientific instruments, the device, called *Sputnik* by the Soviets, showed their progress in rocketry.

The man on the street was quick to put two and two together: If the commies could fire a ball so easily into space, could they not also lob a bomb into America's back yard? The apparent answer was discomforting. However, U.S. scientists had for several years been working on a space experiment similar to the *Sputnik* project. In the early 1950s, small rockets packed with instruments were lifted by balloons through the first ten to fifteen miles of earth's atmosphere, then fired to heights of sixty miles or more. But because the army, the air force, and civilians all were working on separate rocket projects, progress was slow. Nevertheless, on January 31, 1958, less than four months after the launch of *Sputnik*, *Explorer I* became the first American satellite to be placed into orbit. The public was ecstatic.

At the same time, Eisenhower appointed the first special assistant to the president for science and technology. James R. Killian, president of the Massachusetts Institute of Technology, and his assistants put together long-range plans for everything from the Apollo landing on the moon to several orbiting astronomical observatories. Congress quickly passed the National Defense Education Act, designed to get low-cost loan money for schooling into the hands of all students but especially those who showed skill in mathematics or science. Piloted space flight would not begin until 1961, but planning and spending toward that end began in earnest several years earlier.

The Atomic Energy Commission

U.S. scientists convinced the politicians at the end of World War II that civilians, rather than the military, should be in charge of the atomic program. Consequently, a five-member Atomic Energy Commission (AEC) was formed in 1946 to direct modernization of early facilities, to plan and construct atomic power plants, and to design and build weapons. "The biggest single construction job in history" was a 1950s AEC undertaking, on the Savannah River separating Georgia and South Carolina. Plutonium and other materials for bombs were produced at the incredibly

expensive plant. Two other large facilities, Rocky Flats near Denver and a weapons laboratory in Livermore, California, also were established.

Atomic power for war and peace was a major expenditure. It also was in a frightening corner of everybody's mind. Yet daily events confirming the fears were few and far between. The most common emblem of atomic power came to be the black-and-

The U.S. Army's Jupiter-C rocket blasts off from Cape Canaveral in January 1958, propelling America's first satellite, Explorer I, *into space. In July of that year, Congress allotted millions of dollars for the creation of the National Aeronautics and Space Agency (NASA).*

yellow civil defense signs posted outside schools and other public buildings. The signs were on all structures deemed fit for fallout shelters in the event of atomic attack. Many of the chosen buildings also were the sites of caches of food, to be eaten in the event the occupants could not go above ground. Schoolchildren all over the country cringed under their desks or in hallways or basements as part of civil defense air raid drills. What did such frightening drills do to impressionable young minds?

Primarily, it gave them the false notion that they could happily survive World War III, even if U.S. and Soviet arsenals were emptied during the

The world's first nuclear-powered submarine, the Nautilus, *slides out of the shipyard at the Electric Boat division of the General Dynamics Corporation, and into the Thames River, in Groton, Connecticut, in January 1954.*

battle. Much of the civil defense was left to the states, with the federal government producing manuals and creating civilian organizations. "What to Do in Case of an Atomic Bomb Attack" became as familiar to Americans as today's "The Seven Signs of Cancer." Hiding behind a thick wall would save you from radioactivity, according to the instructions, "even if you were close" to the blast. Meanwhile, volunteer paramilitary groups such as the Civil Air Patrol scanned the skies every night for incoming enemy craft.

Scanning the skies did funny things to some people. Beginning in 1952 and continuing on and off to the present, Americans began to detect strange objects in the heavens. Flying saucers, described variously as small, huge, illuminated, glowing, flashing, spinning, afire, landing, and taking off were reported wherever anxious citizens looked aloft. The popular media reported these Unidentified Flying Objects, or UFOs, without making judgments, and the consensus was that the saucers were a secret military project. As the years passed, the reports included a number of folks who claimed to have been taken aboard the craft by aliens. As if the Soviets and Chinese weren't pesky enough, the United States was apparently being harassed by Martians!

Frightening Mishaps

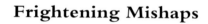

Civil defense drills and UFO sightings proved to be less frightening than the numerous accidents involving atomic power or weapons. In 1958, for example, a U.S. Air Force B-47 carrying an atomic weapon caught fire at an unnamed American

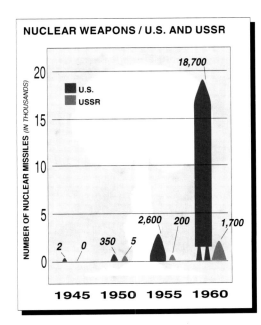

NUCLEAR WEAPONS / U.S. AND USSR

Clandestine Tests

Actually, the United States was quite effective at keeping secrets. Not until late 1993 did the federal government admit that it conducted more than two hundred secret nuclear tests in the Nevada desert beginning in about 1950. The only civilians who were aware of the tests were ranchers whose sheep died as a result of radiation exposure and the residents of tiny towns such as St. George, Utah, about 150 miles east of the test site. People there were exposed to fallout from a 1953 accident that caused high numbers of deaths from leukemia and other cancers in later years. In fairness, less was known about the dangers of radiation then than now.

But there is no excuse for 239 separate experiments, conducted by the U.S. Army and others, on innocent civilians that frequently involved radiation. For example, radioactive clouds were pumped into the atmosphere from Hanford, Washington, so that fallout could be studied. On the other side of the country, retarded boys in Massachusetts were fed radioactive food for ten years, beginning in 1946, to see what effect such a diet would have on human beings. The study was done with parental consent, but radiation was never mentioned. As the Cold War intensified, army personnel experimented in other ways, smashing light bulbs filled with billions of apparently harmless bacteria in crowded subway stations in New York City and on city beaches. In San Francisco, Stanford University hospital patients became infected by airborne bacteria and at least one died as a result. Prisoners often were irradiated without their knowledge and were not given any follow-up care.

base overseas, probably in Spain. The aircraft burned for seven hours, resulting in contamination of the area but not in an atomic explosion. Afterward, the military removed the wreckage and the asphalt beneath it, greatly reducing the amount of radioactivity. A relatively small hydrogen test on the tiny Pacific island of Runit in 1958 failed to detonate, instead spreading dangerous plutonium all over the island. The site was so contaminated that it was deemed fit only as a burial site for radioactive material.

Despite such mishaps, handling of dangerous substances appeared to be in better hands in the U.S. than in several other countries. In 1957, for example, a fire at a plutonium plant in northern England spread contamination across the countryside. And in a vast chemical explosion that same year in Kasli, in the USSR, thousands of people were irradiated and many died. The U.S. government learned about the hushed-up Soviet tragedy belatedly from a defector.

(Left) Despite the fears of the Pentagon, the United States kept well ahead of the Soviet Union in the nuclear arms race throughout the fifties.

"We have beaten you to the moon, but you have beaten us in sausage making."

Nikita Khrushchev in Des Moines, 1959

What Should Be Told?

While schoolchildren were drilled to hide under their desks in the event of atomic attack, the civil defense headquarters in New York proudly displayed this deluxe fallout shelter complete with wall-to-wall carpeting and television. Here, it is used by Mr. and Mrs. Nathaniel H. Schaffaud and their children, Diane and Eric. The shelter was designed to be built above ground so that it could double as a family room during peacetime.

The issues of atomic weaponry and world communism drove editorial writers to distraction. If they told their readers that they could survive weapons of mass destruction, that meant the enemy could survive bombardment, too. If writers dismissed the threat of communism, they risked creating an apathetic public that might not want to spend billions for defense. On the other hand, if they portrayed the Soviets as invincible, the public might feel defeated long before a war even began.

Herman Kahn, director of a think tank, had a curious outlook on the matter. He said that Americans who thought nuclear war to be suicidal were crazy. According to Kahn, who spoke almost cheerfully, "If twenty million Americans were killed, there would be two hundred million survivors." Those who had read John Hersey's award-winning book, *Hiroshima*, or who had followed accounts of the destructive force of the two bombs dropped on Japan in 1945 were less optimistic. They saw that, in many cases, the lucky people were the ones who had been killed instantly in the deadly blasts. Those who survived faced physical and emotional agony, as well as the very real possibility of passing on the effects of the bombs to future generations.

Looking back, the automatic acceptance of nuclear weapons by the popular press is frightening. Major periodicals such as *Colliers, Life, Look, Reader's Digest,* and the *Saturday Evening Post* ran articles such as "Atomic Weapons Will Save Money." The author of this optimistic *Look* magazine piece proudly pointed out that atomic weapons are "one of the cheapest forms of destruction known to man." Others endorsed weapons production as a means of preventing war. Morality aside, no one in the mass media gave a second thought to such a scary point of view.

Voices of Dissent

Was there anyone during the decade who questioned the existence of nuclear weapons? There was, but dissent was stifled by people like U.S. Senator Joseph McCarthy. His permanent investigations subcommittee threatened to deny civil liberties to anyone not supporting the country's military policies. In other words, those who protested against nuclear testing could be jailed indefinitely without being charged with a crime. Dissenters were accused of being either Communists or naive about how the world worked. Nevertheless, a few groups, such as the Catholic Workers, the War Resisters League, numerous clergy, and others, bravely staged protests, trespassed into nuclear-test zones, and issued statements condemning the use of the bomb.

Among the more effective groups was the Committee for Nuclear Information (CNI), formed in 1958 at Washington University in St. Louis, Missouri. This nonpartisan organization of scientists was formed to provide objective technical information in response to public fears of radiation from weapons tests. One of CNI's most attention-getting efforts involved collecting thousands of human baby teeth that showed traces of strontium-90, a product of fallout. Other major critics of nuclear power came from the U.S. weapons program itself. These scientists had discovered frightening consequences of prolonged radiation on human beings, but their research was suppressed.

Despite their awesome force, nuclear weapons had limitations. Many Americans advocated using atom bombs in the Korean War whenever the tide turned in favor of the North Koreans and the Communist Chinese. But dropping a bomb on the war-torn peninsula would have endangered U.S. and other friendly troops. It probably would have caused massive unrest in antinuclear Japan; it would have made no real dent in the number of soldiers the Chinese could furnish, and would make America appear trigger-happy to its United Nations allies. More than 54,000 U.S. soldiers died during the Korean conflict, and twice that number were wounded. It's safe to say that a nuclear exchange in Korea would have killed many times those numbers. The ultimate decision not to drop the bomb was made, of course, by the very same person who approved bombing Hiroshima and Nagasaki — President Harry S Truman.

Atoms for Peace

If there was any hope concerning nuclear power, it came in a speech by Dwight Eisenhower, the man who succeeded Truman. Speaking at the United Nations in 1953, Ike proposed a plan he called Atoms for Peace. Aware that the United States no longer had a worldwide monopoly on atomic power, Eisenhower proposed the joint exploration of peaceful uses for the atom. This more cooperative stance was followed by the U.S. Atomic Energy Act of 1954. It opened the door for international nuclear cooperation and for the development of atomic power by private industry, in conjunction with the Atomic Energy Commission. The major result of this renewed look was a boom in government and civilian spending. Ground was broken in September 1954 for the first of many nuclear power stations.

One of the reasons the government decided to share responsibility with private industry was economic. Eisenhower had pledged to cut the federal budget, and atomic power plants were expensive to develop. An

"Know the Bomb's True Dangers. Know the Steps You Can Take to Escape Them! — You Can Survive."

Government pamphlet, 1950

Engineers and technicians supervise the fifty-eight ton, multi-million-dollar nuclear core of America's first full-scale atomic electric generating station exclusively for civilian use. Atomic power seemed to be the answer to everyone's energy problems in the fifties, when the potential dangers to people and the environment were either not known, or were suppressed by the government.

unforeseen problem was what to do with the growing amount of radioactive waste such power plants would generate. Spent nuclear fuel and other waste began to mount before the 1950s ended, and as early as 1958, leaks from storage drums were reported in Hanford, Washington. The Joint Committee on Atomic Energy's answer to the problem was to hold hearings, deciding in 1959 that waste did not pose an insurmountable problem. More than three decades later, as nuclear dump sites bulge with tons of waste, the committee's judgment seems much less optimistic.

CHAPTER 8
Hollywood and the Arts

For a while in the 1950s, it seemed that the bright lights of Hollywood were fading. In 1951, the motion picture business produced more than 400 films; in 1960, only 154 were created. Neither the quality nor the quantity of actors had diminished, so what was the trouble? There were several reasons, among the most important being the incredible popularity of television. TV was seen by movie moguls as giving the public for free what it was used to paying for at the box office to see. Consequently, the people who invested their money

in Hollywood became more cautious. They refused to bankroll any script that was not a sure thing. One result was a decade of sameness on the silver screen.

The motion picture business had other problems, and one of them was politics. Numerous creative people in Hollywood were would-be intellectuals and various kinds of left-leaning free thinkers. When communism surged in popularity during the 1930s, these people had attended meetings, listened to speakers, even contributed money. Though virtually no one was

Movies like From Here to Eternity, *with its smoldering beach scene between Burt Lancaster and Deborah Kerr, were considered rather daring but they helped pack in the audiences. Lancaster (right) can be seen here with Frank Sinatra (left) and Montgomery Clift.*

still a Communist sympathizer by 1950 (knowing, by then, of the willingness of dictator Josef Stalin to sacrifice his own people), previous connections would come back to haunt some of Hollywood's most talented people.

Writers in particular were blacklisted — their names were placed on a list of people the studios were not supposed to hire. Worse, many were called before congressional committees such as HUAC and forced to tell who among their friends had ever attended Communist gatherings or still showed Communist sympathy. Few in the business could trust their associates. Talented writers such as Dalton Trumbo, whose name was on the blacklist, wrote under assumed names in order to make a living. Actors such as Aldo Ray and Sterling Hayden didn't work for years, all because they attended the wrong meetings as kids. Few in Hollywood stood up to the blacklist or to the anti-communist ferrets for fear of losing their jobs.

There were other concerns. Federal authorities forced the motion picture studios to sell their chains of movie theaters. The government rightly believed that owning both production and distribution ends of the business encouraged monopolies. One result was that the smaller, less popular theaters in small towns all over the country flickered and went dark. The star system, wherein young actors and actresses worked their way to the top, also was in danger of being eclipsed. The huge exposure from television resulted in instant stardom for everyone on TV, from Fess Parker (who played Davy Crockett) to Annette Funicello of "The Mickey Mouse Club" to Jack Webb of the police series "Dragnet."

Major studios became financially shaky as independent filmmakers created meaningful movies at a fraction of the cost to do so at Metro-Goldwyn-Mayer or Twentieth Century Fox. These mavericks often dealt with sexual, racial, and other subjects the big studios considered taboo. Some studios dipped into their archives, distributing prints of old movies to television stations for airing late at night and on weekend afternoons. Old films heightened interest in 1930s actors such as George Raft, Mae West, and Jimmy Cagney, but did little to lure more people into theaters. RKO in particular did a thriving business in the old horror movies of Lon Chaney and other frightening folks. They were seen on local late-night television under names such as "Wide-Scream Theater," usually featuring a vampirelike host.

High Tech Special Effects

The movie magnates decided to deliver the kinds of things the TV screen could not. Among the most talked about was 3-D. Three-dimensional pictures looked like two films running on top of each other to the naked eye. But to moviegoers wearing paper-and-cellophane glasses, the screen appeared to have real depth — a third dimension. Directors focused entire movies around the fact that arrows or cannonballs or monsters coming toward the camera appeared as if they were going to fly directly into the audience. The 3-D craze opened with *Bwana Devil* in 1952 and lasted for a couple of years until people realized that they were buying tickets only for a few minutes of special effects. By

"One nice thing about television. You don't have to pick out where to look."

New Yorker Cartoon by Gardner Rea, 1951

"They'll wear toilet seats around their necks if you give 'em what they want to see."

Bill Thomas, on 3-D glasses, 1952

Marlon Brando.

The Nebraska-born son of a traveling salesman and a woman who was never able to realize acting ambitions, Marlon Brando was a rebel and an individual in a time when both of these attributes were in short supply.

Brando was a "method" actor. That is, he recalled emotions and experiences from his own past to use in whatever role he was playing. His talent first gained wide attention in 1947 in the Tennessee Williams play, *A Streetcar Named Desire*. He overwhelmed audiences and critics, and his success led to many Hollywood roles.

No matter what the character, Brando was effective on screen. His acting, which could include mumbling rather than carefully spoken dialogue, is said to have revolutionized the movies. His natural behavior in front of the camera influenced a generation of players. Yet he could speak as sharply as the next actor when he chose, proving it by playing Mark Antony in the 1951 film of Shakespeare's *Julius Caesar*.

His other films in the fifties included *Viva Zapata* and *A Streetcar Named Desire* in 1951, *The Wild One* in 1954, and *On the Waterfront,* also in 1954. His unique ability to portray a revolutionary, an outcast, a punchy fighter, or the leader of a motorcycle gang wowed both suburban teenagers and big-city intellectuals alike.

Leather-jacketed Marlon Brando helps promote his classic, The Wild One, *in this 1954 poster for the film.*

Brando's personal life has always been somewhat stormy. His marriage to actress Anna Kashfi was short and nasty, and he has frequently taken up causes that made him seem a half-baked activist. But he has never been less than great in a movie. He proved his range in later films, acting in and directing an immortal cowboy movie, *One-Eyed Jacks*, in 1961, and serving in a supporting but magnetic role as Don Corleone in *The Godfather* in 1972. He also starred in 1973's sexually explicit *Last Tango in Paris* and played the superhero's father in the 1978 adventure movie, *Superman*, perhaps to prove he could take himself less seriously.

Together with James Dean, Elvis Presley, and other musicians and hipsters, Brando's style served as a model for rebellious male America during the Eisenhower years.

the middle of the decade, 3-D technology was history.

Another special effects item was Cinerama, which featured a large screen and sound that emerged from speakers placed all around the audience. It, too, was exciting, but the only Cinerama theaters were in big cities. Nevertheless, for a few years theatergoers paid to watch Lowell Thomas travelogues and similar spectacles on the bigger screens with the richer sound tracks. CinemaScope and stereophonic sound meant better picture quality and the ability of a sound or voice to follow its source back and forth across the screen. The French introduced a better movie camera, and color became the rule rather than the exception by the end of the decade. None of the effects contributed to artistic quality, however.

The Big Stars

Who did the public line up to see? Leading actors included Humphrey Bogart, Marlon Brando, Gary Cooper, Kirk Douglas, Charlton Heston, Rock Hudson, Burt Lancaster, James Stewart, and John Wayne. Top actresses were June Allison, Doris Day, Ava Gardner, Susan Hayward, Audrey Hepburn, Judy Holliday, Grace Kelly, Vivien Leigh, and Joanne Woodward. A great film could succeed without a top star, as *Marty*, with Ernest Borgnine playing a butcher looking for love, proved in 1955. A gritty black-and-white film with superior acting could lure people away from TV, as William Holden showed in 1953 in *Stalag 17*. Fans were suckers for stereotypes, as Judy Holliday confirmed in *Born Yesterday*, a 1950 movie about a dumb blonde played by a talented one.

Westerns were highly popular, with *High Noon,* starring Gary Cooper, taking the Oscar for Best Picture in 1952. Spectacles such as *Ben Hur* in 1959, starring Charlton Heston, or *The King and I* in 1956, with Deborah Kerr and Yul Brynner, won large male and female audiences. Teenagers, always eager to get out of the house, were treated to monster flicks such as *Them,* which featured ants the size of houses, or *Invasion of the Body Snatchers,* where look-alike humans came out of pods to take over the earth. The movie served as an allegory for the

> *"Talk low, talk slow and don't say too much."*
>
> Actor John Wayne

Grace Kelly fulfilled everyone's dreams about the fairytale lifestyles of America's most glamorous actresses. Born in Philadelphia in 1929, she cut short her successful movie career to marry Prince Rainier of Monaco in 1956, to become a real-life princess. Before her retirement, Kelly starred in Dial M for Murder, Rear Window *(both 1954), and* The Country Girl *(also 1954), opposite Bing Crosby, for which she won an Academy Award.*

dangerous ease by which murderous Communists could subvert and infiltrate American society.

The hundreds of outdoor drive-in movie theaters solved the problem of babysitting — millions of small children fell asleep in the back seat as their parents watched the feature through the windshields of a Nash, DeSoto, or Packard. Drive-ins became known as "passion pits" among teenage kids, who experimented with elementary sex in their cars.

Throughout the decade, the American public enjoyed a British transplant. Long lines formed for movies by Alfred Hitchcock, who directed a number of scary movies that nevertheless showed frequent signs of humor and even romance. They included *The Trouble with Harry, Rear Window, The Birds, North by Northwest,* and others. Hitchcock had no trouble signing up stars the calibre of Cary Grant, Grace Kelly, Shirley MacLaine, and James Stewart. At the opposite extreme were the teenage exploitation movies, which pandered to the juvenile-delinquent fantasies of high school kids. These low-budget, black-and-white films often featured a rock star singing the theme song and bore titles that promised more than they delivered such as *Eighteen and Anxious, Explosive Generation,* and *Reform School Girl.*

Women and Minorities

The roles of women in these movies weren't terrible, though some were so relentlessly perky they had little relationship to reality. Doris Day

Deborah Kerr thrilled audiences in a smash-hit spectacle in 1959, starring with Yul Brynner in Walter Lang's musical, The King and I. *Kerr played a visiting English woman, educating the King of Siam in the sophisticated ways of the West.*

Sidney Poitier was one of the first African-American actors to gain serious recognition. Here, he stars with Ruby Dee and Diana Sands in the 1959 Broadway production of A Raisin in the Sun, *which was about the aspirations of a black family. The hit production was made into a movie, also starring Poitier and Sands, in 1961.*

must have had bad days, but theatergoers never knew it, as the star of romantic comedies went from a smile to a song to boundless optimism all within a single scene. In more serious films, much was made over a woman's ability to influence a man to make the right decision. Women also could be assertive, as Eva Marie Saint's character showed, influencing Marlon Brando's character in *On the Waterfront* in 1954. But perhaps vulnerability, as displayed by Marilyn Monroe in a series of sexy comedies, was the female personality trait most admired by the people who ran Hollywood. Older actresses such as Katharine Hepburn still commanded attention, and Rosalind Russell wowed audiences in 1959 in *Auntie Mame.*

With a few important exceptions, minorities were either not seen at all or shown through the eyes of white producers and directors during the decade. American Indians probably suffered the most, confined as they were to halting sentences, primitive emotions, and wagon train attacks. Blacks simply weren't seen very often, though exceptional actors could command attention by their presence. The best example is Sidney Poitier, chained to fellow convict Tony Curtis in 1958 in *The Defiant Ones,* a story about two work-gang escapees and how they learned to tolerate one another. The industry by the end of the decade was creaking open to African-American actors in more and better roles.

Except for German Volkswagens, Japanese transistor radios, and Italian pizza, Americans didn't pay much attention to foreign goods. The exception was the movies, where numerous foreign stars won over American audiences. Notable examples are Elizabeth Taylor and Joan Collins from Britain, Sophia Loren and Gina Lollobrigida from Italy, Anita Ekberg from Sweden. Each one added to a reputation earned in Europe. Two foreigners, British actor David Niven and Mexican comedian Cantinflas, were international hits in the 1956 film version of the Jules Verne book, *Around the World in Eighty Days.* Niven won Best Actor two years later in a modest drama, *Separate Tables.* Simone Signoret, the veteran French star, took home an Oscar for Best Actress in 1959 for a vivid performance in *Room at the Top.*

Cantinflas. (1911-1993)

Cantinflas was the Charlie Chaplin of Latin America. Besides being a gifted actor, he was also a social activist and a humanitarian during a period when many Spanish-speaking people in the western hemisphere were being victimized by uncaring or vicious governments.

A Mexican native whose real name was Mario Moreno, Cantinflas's career spanned half a century. He made a total of forty-nine films. Unfortunately, the fact that most were in Spanish prevented them from being seen widely in the United States.

In his second film, *Ni Sangre Ni Arena (Neither Blood Nor Sand),* in 1941, Cantinflas portrayed a toreador who gets the best of the bull despite incredible incompetence. The part became such a Cantinflas trademark that he was forced to reproduce the zany bullfight every year in benefit performances.

Luckily, American audiences saw the nutty toreador in Jules Verne's *Around the World in Eighty Days*, a 1956 movie that also starred David Niven. Cantinflas stole the show as Passepartout, Niven's valet, while Niven played the hero, Phileas Fogg. The Mexican actor tipped alert U.S. filmgoers to the fact that there was a whole talented world outside the confines of 1950s American cinema.

Cantinflas's later films were often funny but were more consistently political. He advocated social reform and became a hero to Mexico's masses. His sympathetic screen characters combined with his generosity to become a virtual one-man welfare system for the poor and homeless who lived in the slums of Mexico City.

Hundreds of poor persons lined up outside his door each day. He gave away some $175,000 a year for several years. Meanwhile, he constructed more than sixty apartment buildings, selling units to poor families for a fraction of their true worth.

A founder of the Mexican Cinema Production Workers Union, the actor died in 1993 in Mexico City and was mourned by the entire western hemisphere.

Mexican actor Cantinflas (left) became world famous after he starred with David Niven in Around the World in Eighty Days.

Good Writing

Those who believe the 1950s were mediocre should check library shelves. The greats — Faulkner, Hemingway, Steinbeck — were still writing, and a number of today's best were launching their careers. Ernest Hemingway brought forth his timeless *The Old Man and the Sea* in 1953. William Faulkner's *A Fable*, though not of the stature of *The Sound and the Fury*, showed that alcohol had not wiped out the Mississippi writer's talent. John Steinbeck continued to produce noteworthy work in the 1950s, including *East of Eden* in 1952. Other writers who made headlines included Herman Wouk, with *The Caine Mutiny* (1951), MacKinlay Kantor, with Pulitzer Prize-winning *Andersonville* (1956), and James Agee, with *A Death in the Family* (1958).

One of the most popular nonfiction books of the decade was Senator John F. Kennedy's *Profiles in Courage*, written in 1955. Equally sought after

"[In San Antonio] the main question is: Should books on the public library shelves whose authors are . . . identified as Communist . . . be branded with a red stamp?"

Stanley Walker, "Book Branding," 1953

> *"[The] Beat Generation [are] hip without being slick, intelligent without being corny."*
>
> Jack Kerouac, 1958

was *The Spirit of St. Louis*, the 1954 Charles A. Lindbergh autobiography. Writers whose first books came out in the 1950s included James Baldwin, Saul Bellow, John Cheever, J. D. Salinger, William Styron, and John Updike. Expatriate writers such as Russian Vladimir Nabokov successfully made the switch to English during the decade. Women writers with large followings included Kay Boyle, black poet Gwendolyn Brooks, Mary McCarthy, Carson McCullers, Flannery O'Connor, and Eudora Welty.

Intense Drama

Dramatists had a lot of impact. Although Tennessee Williams' *A Streetcar Named Desire* and Arthur Miller's *Death of a Salesman* were written in the late 1940s, they continued to wow 1950s audiences. Eugene

Allen Ginsberg (right), with Peter Orlovsky, on a double-sided bench in the Place St. Germain des Prés, Paris, 1956.

Allen Ginsberg.

Allen Ginsberg's incredible poem, *Howl* (1956), did almost as much for the 1950s as *Uncle Tom's Cabin* did for the 1860s. On one hand it freed literate Americans from their love of starchy, academic writing; on the other, it helped them turn their backs on the political conservatism so popular at the time. *Howl*, which lamented the wasting of fine minds, became the anthem of the Beat Generation.

Beats, or Beatniks, were poets, writers, and artists living in places such as New York City's Greenwich Village and in San Francisco. They listened to Ginsberg draw on influences such as poets William Blake and Walt Whitman to paint a fractured, often discouraging picture of America.

The New Jersey native with the radical views grew up the son of middle-class, Jewish parents, and attended Columbia University in New York City. There, as World War II was ending, he was influenced by drugs, left-wing politics, homosexuality, Far Eastern religions, free-form poetry, chaos in general, and teachers and fellow students who thought as he did. Ginsberg decided as a young man to dedicate himself to art. He traveled widely, keeping journals and writing poetry while he worked as everything from a kitchen helper to a market researcher. Along the way, he absorbed a great deal of knowledge about his native land.

Ginsberg moved between the two coasts after studying Buddhism in Asia. He was welcomed at progressive colleges and not issued invitations by others. By the middle 1960s, with the hippie counterculture movement in full flower on the coasts, young and radical Americans were looking to Ginsberg for leadership. Ever the entertainer, he showed up for rallies and demonstrations but cavorted in an Uncle Sam suit rather than issuing instructions on how to revolt.

Nevertheless, Ginsberg, along with writers such as Jack Kerouac and William Burroughs, kept progressive art alive during a decade when it might otherwise have died out for lack of interest. His poems continue to be read and praised by critics.

Martha Graham. (1895-1991)

At a time in life when other people plan their retirement, Martha Graham really hit her stride. The dance teacher created more than 150 ballets over her long career, the best among them *Letter to the World* (1940), *Appalachian Spring* (1944), *Night Journey* (1947), *Diversion of Angels* (1948), *Clytemnestra* (1958), and *Acrobats of God* (1960). The latter was created during Graham's sixty-sixth year.

The native of small-town Allegheny, Pennsylvania, Graham was one of the founders of American modern dance. She rejected formal dance training, creating instead a "Graham" dance technique that was much looser and more expressive than classical ballet. Her dancers fell to the floor, extended their limbs wildly, and contracted them unexpectedly. To audiences used to European formality, a Graham performance was an unequalled visual treat.

Graham tried hard in her ballets to show character, motivation, and psychological complexities. Her studio in New York City became a hub for hopeful young dancers, many of whom migrated there upon learning of the choreographer's willingness to innovate. In later years, companies employing her techniques were started in London and in Israel.

O'Neill completed *Long Day's Journey into Night* in 1957, while Lillian Hellman basked in the glow of great reviews of several plays, including *The Children's Hour.* Tennessee Williams confirmed his talent in 1955 with *Cat on a Hot Tin Roof,* and Richard Rodgers, Oscar Hammerstein II, and Joshua Logan won raves for their 1950 musical fantasy, *South Pacific.* But the decade's most wrenching play was adapted by Frances Goodrich and Albert Hackett from the true story of a child who died in a Nazi death camp in their collaboration, *The Diary of Anne Frank* in 1956.

Further filling the stages, dance companies flourished during the decade. The New York City Ballet Company was thriving, while independent companies, such as Martha Graham's, influenced dance styles here and abroad. Agnes De Mille was winding up a long career of staging musicals in every part of the country. Doris Humphrey directed her own company until she was crippled by arthritis. And several women continued to dance their way to critical acclaim, including Ruth St. Denis with her "American Dance" program, and American Indian Maria Tallchief, who became famous for her Stravinsky-Diaghilev-Balanchine "Firebird." Black dancers, sometimes suffering discrimination, found an important new outlet for their talent

"A man should be jailed for telling lies to the young."

Lillian Hellman, playwright

Maria Callas. (1923-1977)

Among opera singers, Maria Callas stands at the pinnacle. She was a diva, a prima donna, a person upon whom all eyes were riveted and ears cocked towards whenever she swept on stage.

Callas was born Maria Calogeropoulou in New York City. Her parents were of Greek descent, and they sacrificed to pay for her early training, much of which took place in Europe. She made her debut in Athens in 1941 in the title role of Puccini's *Tosca*. She played and sang the part many times to rapt audiences; operagoers ceased to think of anyone else in the role.

It is tempting to think of her only as a beautiful and high-strung singer, living for love and art, but she was capable of singing an array of operas, from Wagner to Cherubini and Donizetti. In fact, she mastered a large number of roles in a professional career that spanned part of four decades. Despite her fame, she wasn't the frequent subject of tabloid newspapers. She spent much more time in Europe than in the U.S. after World War II, becoming a naturalized Greek citizen in 1966.

Some critics have said that her voice was not perfect but her insight into the music and her stage presence were what made her world famous. One claimed, "She is one of the very few singers of whom one would use the word genius." Unfortunately, she died at the age of fifty-four, still at the peak of her career.

in 1958. That year, Alvin Ailey created the American Dance Theatre, which featured all-black casts and dance styles that were both original and visually exciting.

Intellectual Enrichment

The United States benefited from the flow of refugees from Germany before and after World War II. Those who made real contributions to American thought included Hannah Arendt. She wrote *The Origins of Totalitarianism* in 1951 and *The Human Condition* in 1958, becoming the first woman full professor at Princeton. A political scientist and a philosopher, she studied moral issues and distrusted American conformists. Another thoughtful refugee was Paul Tillich. He taught at Union Theological Seminary in New York City, where he looked for the connections between traditional Christianity and twentieth century culture.

The decade witnessed the opening of one of the most unusual architectural structures ever designed, and the death of its creator. Frank Lloyd Wright was commissioned in 1943 to design the Guggenheim Museum in New York City. The art showplace was finally completed in 1959, and consisted of a multilayered spiral that

Collage, *by Willem de Kooning, 1950, displays the artist's characteristically flourishing blend of color and brushwork. Kooning, a Dutch immigrant, had arrived in America in 1926 as a stowaway on a cattle boat. By the fifties, his unique style had earned him a reputation as one of America's leading abstract expressionists.*

viewers of art followed as they walked toward the top or the ground floor of the building. The structure remains one of the most memorable on earth, as do many of Wright's earlier projects. A genius whose finances and personal life were sometimes in disarray, Wright died in 1959. Along with Ludwig Mies Van Der Rohe, whose trademark was steel and glass skyscrapers with "ribbon windows," Wright made the mid-twentieth century an important architectural period.

Visual art was dominated by people like Willem de Kooning and Jackson Pollock. De Kooning was a native of Holland who came to New York City and helped it become the world's art capital. His abstract expressionist style combined planned and accidental effects with slashing and splashy brushstrokes. As he grew older, his work became more erotic and bizarre. Pollock, by contrast, was a native New Yorker who studied in the 1930s under Thomas Hart Benton and then became impressed with the use of spray guns

and airbrushes in art — tools that lent themselves to the abstract. He was influenced by Picasso and others, using black extensively on canvasses that appeared to have no beginning or end. Peggy Guggenheim, who doled out money for the museum designed by Frank Lloyd Wright, and which bears her name, was his patron. Pollock died in a car crash in 1956.

The New York art world carried on, as women such as Pollock's wife, Lee Krasner, along with Helen Frankenthaler and Elaine de Kooning, established solid reputations. Popular artists nationwide were Georgia O'Keeffe, who worked in Arizona, and Andrew Wyeth, who was both an illustrator and a fine artist. But the two most popular and widely known artists were Norman Rockwell, who painted likeable, everyday people in folksy situations, and Grandma Moses. Anna Mary Robertson Moses began painting at the age of sixty-seven and was featured all over the country in shows of her simple rural scenes.

> *"No house should ever be on any hill or on anything. It should be of the hill, belonging to it, so hill and house could live together each the happier for the other."*
>
> Frank Lloyd Wright, from his autobiography, 1932

CHAPTER 9
TV's the Thing

Before 1945, television simply did not exist for most people in the United States. Yet, by 1950, 4.4 million American families owned TV sets, and by 1956, they were buying them at the rate of twenty thousand a day! By 1960, 90 percent of American homes had at least one television. This single invention introduced some astounding changes to American culture in the fifties, altering not just family entertainment and the communication of news but the ways in which people looked, acted, and even thought.

The Golden Age of Television

By 1950, four major networks were on the air — NBC, CBS, ABC, and the DuMont Television Network. Although the DuMont network only lasted until 1955, it owned stations in New York, Pittsburgh, and Washington, D.C. It also provided a good deal of exposure for such stars as Jackie Gleason and Bishop Fulton J. Sheen before it folded.

Television technology also continued to be developed. By the late 1940s, scientists and engineers had been closing in on the invention of color television, and in the fifties, inventors were working hard on other tools that would continue to revolutionize television technology — inventions such as videotape, home video systems, and satellite transmission.

Even more miraculous in the early fifties was the exceptional group of people who came together to create the first nationally broadcast shows. It was their efforts that created what has come to be known as the golden age of television. There were no pretaped programs during this period in television history; everything was live. The potential catastrophes of putting on a live show — the flubbed lines, stage fright, accidents on the set — added to the spirit of adventure and discovery.

Many of the first television viewers were affluent city people who regularly attended the theater, so drama became an important part of TV programming right from the beginning. Many of the first TV dramas were recreations of existing Broadway plays, but soon networks were hiring writers to create original dramas expressly for TV. Many great producers and directors, such as Fred Coe, Fred Zinneman, and George Roy Hill, got started working on such series as "Studio One," "The U.S. Steel Hour," "Kraft Television Theater," "The Alcoa Hour," and "Pulitzer Prize Playhouse." So did a number of important writers: Paddy Chayefsy, who wrote the classic drama "Marty;" Rod Serling, who wrote "Requiem for a Heavyweight" before going on to write the "Twilight Zone" and "Night Gallery" anthologies; J. P. Miller, Gore Vidal, William Gibson, and many others started on TV.

According to director John Frankenheimer, as soon as programs began to be pretaped, the people involved no longer felt compelled to give each take

> *"If the television craze continues with the present level of programs, we are destined to have a nation of morons."*
>
> Boston University President Daniel Marsh, 1950

their best shot. They knew that if anything went wrong, it could simply be retaped. The invention of magnetic tape, they believed, destroyed not only live television, but the true magic of television's golden age.

Comedy–Variety Shows

Drama was by no means the only exciting and imaginative programming in the early fifties. Adult comedy-variety shows like Milton Berle's "Texaco Star Theater" were immediate hits. In fact, Berle became known affectionately as "Mr. Television" and "Uncle Miltie." His "Texaco Star Theater" was aired on Tuesday nights, getting its start when most people still didn't own TV sets. The program was so popular that those few people on a given city block who did own sets would put them in their front windows with the screens facing the street. Half the rest of the block would gather (sometimes fifty people or more) to watch Uncle Miltie clowning on camera, glued to the action even though they couldn't hear the sound.

George Burns and Gracie Allen were one of the first comedy teams to make the transition from radio to television, just as they had made the earlier transition from vaudeville to radio. Sid Ceasar was another established comedian who hosted his own popular variety program, "Your Show of Shows." Ceasar was particularly well known for playing nutty professor characters like Professor Sigmund von Fraidy Katz, an expert on mountain climbing, and Dr. Heinrich von Heartburn, an expert on marriage. His show also had some extremely talented writers, including Mel Brooks,

If you wanted to survive in show business, you had to move with the times. Gracie Allen and George Burns successfully made the transition from radio to television in the fifties with their comedy act. In this typical scene, Gracie berates George in the kitchen.

Neil Simon, and Woody Allen, all of whom would later write and direct movies of their own. Other gifted comedians who hosted comedy-variety shows in the fifties included Jackie Gleason and Red Skelton.

But you didn't have to be a comedian or even have an obvious talent to get your own TV show in those days. A perfect example is the grandaddy of all variety shows, "The Ed Sullivan Show," originally called "The Toast of the Town." Sullivan's irritable voice and hunched over appearance may have made him an almost laughable TV host figure, but his show was the only place where a viewer could watch every kind of star entertainment, from the Moiseyev ballet dancers to Elvis Presley or Albert Schweitzer. Other networks tried to duplicate the show's unexplainable success with programs like "Hollywood Palace," but Ed Sullivan was unique.

Successful singers were also given their own variety shows. Perry Como, Dinah Shore, Rosemary Clooney, Andy Williams, and Kate Smith all enjoyed popular success. While they weren't exactly today's music videos, the weekly production numbers on "Your Hit Parade" provided a regular countdown of the country's top billboard hits. A music program aimed at a younger audience, "Dick Clark's American Bandstand," not only featured the week's top hits but asked typical teens to rate the new releases as other teen couples danced on screen.

The Rise of the Sitcom

Some of the very first sitcoms (short for situation comedies), such as "The Jack Benny Show," "Amos 'n' Andy," and "The Goldbergs," were transferred directly from radio. One of the first successful sitcoms written expressly for television was NBC's "Mister Peepers," staring Wally Cox as a mild-mannered science teacher named "Robinson Peepers." Another popular series, "The Honeymooners," starring Jackie Gleason and Art Carney, started as a sketch on Jackie Gleason's variety show and became a series of its own. Phil Silvers starred in a nonfamily sitcom about a scheming army-sergeant con-man named Ernie Bilko on "The Phil Silvers Show," originally called "You'll Never Get Rich." Reruns of many of these early programs can still be seen on daytime TV.

It's been said that watching the half-hour sitcoms of the early fifties was like taking a combined dose of Valium and jelly beans. All was calm; all was sweet. Almost all of them revolved around families in which the Dad went off to some sort of job somewhere, shouting "Hi honey, I'm home!" as he returned each evening to his delightful and appreciative wife and children. "The Adventures of Ozzie and Harriet," "Lassie," "Leave It to Beaver," "Make Room for Daddy," and "Father Knows Best" are all examples of this type of innocent family fun, but probably the classic sitcom of the fifties was "I Love Lucy," starring Lucille Ball and Desi Arnaz as the wacky Lucy and Ricky Ricardo. You can still turn on a TV in virtually any country in the world and see Lucy in a rerun of one of those old episodes, knee-deep in grapes at an Italian vineyard or becoming drunker and drunker as she flubs take after take of a commercial for an absurd alcohol-based health food elixir called Vitameatavegamin.

Lucille Ball. (1911-1989)

Many people have been called television pioneers, but no one was more of an innovator than Lucille Ball.

Born the daughter of an electrician in Jamestown, New York, she left home at the age of fifteen to study acting in Manhattan. Her long legs and flaming red hair earned her a place in several chorus lines, and she migrated to Hollywood to become a supporting actress rather than a high-demand celebrity. Then came network television.

Ball and TV were a strange combination. She was forty years old when her first thirty-minute show, "I Love Lucy," aired. Not widely known or noticed, she had experienced success on radio but could not be called a star. To complicate matters, Ball insisted that her real-life husband, bandleader Desi Arnaz, co-star on the show. It did not matter to her that Arnaz, a Cuban native, mutilated the English language.

The unlikely duo was an immense hit. Along with personalities such as Jack Benny, Milton Berle, and Jackie Gleason, Ball ignited the small tube in homes all across the land. She was willing to humiliate herself in hundreds of ways for laughs, resulting in "I Love Lucy" and its successors being seen nonstop by prime-time viewers from 1951 to 1974.

Her shows reflected many noncontroversial postwar themes — buying a home, going on vacation, puttering in the yard, getting a job. Lucy got out of the kitchen on her show, only to be faced with goofy problems resulting from getting a job as a wrapper of candy, being the mother of schoolchildren, or coping with life as the wife of an entertainer. It's hardly an exaggeration to call Lucille Ball the mother of today's slew of funny young female TV comedians.

Despite his accent, Arnaz played the straight man to Lucy's shenanigans. Looking back, his condescending stage manner bordered on abuse, but life was very different then than now. Off camera, Arnaz was a talented musician but also a hard drinker, a workaholic, and had a weakness for younger women.

Lucille Ball with real-life and TV husband Desi Arnaz, in 1953.

After their divorce in 1960, the weekly comedy became "The Lucy Show" and then "Here's Lucy" before finally ending. Lucy remarried in 1961 and became, as head of Desilu Production, the first woman to run a major film studio.

Ball's trademark facial expressions eventually became too familiar. An obsessive rehearser and a master of timing, she nevertheless was unable to launch a new situation comedy after 1986. Last seen on awards shows, where Oscars and Emmys were passed out to younger successors, Ball and her antics can still be enjoyed on cable television stations as black-and-white reruns.

About the only other TV shows besides sitcoms like "I Love Lucy" that featured women in strong leading roles were the soap operas. The roles that these women played in shows like "As the World Turns" and "The Edge of Night," which both premiered in 1956, were not especially

Most of the top-ten favorite TV programs through the fifties were westerns like "Gunsmoke," which starred James Arness and Amanda Blake, and premiered in 1955. "Gunsmoke" won an Emmy award in 1957 and remains popular among American TV audiences to this day.

good role models, however. The leading characters were usually bitter and unhappily married middle-aged women surrounded by weak-willed and inept men.

Action-Adventure Shows

Like soap operas, action-adventure shows did not really mature into more worthwhile programming until the sixties and seventies. The fifties adventure programs, like "Hawaiian Eye," "Wire Service," "77 Sunset Strip," and "Surfside 6," all featured predictable formula plots in which a detective, aided by a "cute" secretary, girlfriend, or wife, was almost killed by the bad guys in a hair-raising chase scene, then solved the crime and put the creeps behind bars. Rough language and sexual innuendo were not allowed on fifties TV. About the only interest-getting device that was allowed was violence, and producers made sure these shows had plenty of it. Another good example is ABC's "Untouchables," a series that depicted Eliot Ness's bloody gun battles with prohibition bootleggers. It did not premiere until 1959, but quickly blasted its way into television's top ten.

By 1958, the most popular subcategory of action adventure programming was the western. Of the top ten shows rated that year by the Nielsen national index, seven were shoot-'em-ups, including "Wagon Train," "Have Gun Will Travel," "The Rifleman," "Maverick," "Wells Fargo," and "Wyatt Earp." Premiering in 1955, "Gunsmoke" was the longest-running western on television. It starred James Arness as Marshall Matt Dillon and Dennis Weaver as his limping, not-very-bright deputy, Chester B. Goode. Killing was considered wrong in the fifties western, but it was continually depicted anyway. After all, the writers knew that a man's gotta do what a man's gotta do.

Quiz Shows

The daytime and early evening quiz shows that are so popular now were solid prime-time hits in the early fifties. The concept of game shows actually goes back to the early days of radio, when shows like "Stop the Music" and "Break the Bank" were programming staples. They were a natural for television, too, not just because the large prizes they offered captured the public's greedy imagination, but because they were some of the easiest and cheapest programs to produce. Some early game show hits included "I've Got a Secret," on which people would try to stump a celebrity panel with such bizarre confessions as "I saw President Lincoln assassinated;" "The Price is Right," where contestants tried to guess the correct retail price of power boats and living room sets; and "Queen for a Day," on which housewives contested for prizes by telling viewers their tragic tales of woe. On this show, the woman with the most pathetic story was the winner.

One of the key figures in the television quiz show business was a game show host and producer named Jack Barry. He originally starred on such programs as "Tic Tac Dough," "Juvenile Jury," and the children's show "Winky Dink," the program that allowed you to draw on your TV with a magic screen. But Barry was also involved in the production of "Twenty-One," a game show that almost destroyed all the others. A disgruntled contestant accused Barry of rigging the game in favor of another contestant who defeated him in a tense last round in which the stakes were unusually high. The contestant who won, Charles Van Doren, became an admired and popular national celebrity. When he later confessed under examination that Barry had indeed given him the questions and answers for the show on which he won, Barry

found himself in big trouble. Van Doren's confession caused such a scandal that national congressional hearings were held to investigate the allegations. Even President Eisenhower publicly expressed his outrage over the immorality of the scandal.

The president of CBS, Frank Stranton, responded by cancelling most of the game shows his network had scheduled every week, just in case there was any doubt in any viewers' minds that any of these other shows had been rigged. One of the most popular of these cancelled game shows was "The $64,000 Question." The

In the game show "Twenty-One," Charles Van Doren seems to agonize over the question that was to end his reign as quiz champion. He lost to female attorney, Vivienne Nearing, having earned $129,000 over fourteen Monday nights — the largest single amount paid by a TV quiz show at that time. Later the show was proved to have been rigged and Van Doren and producer Jack Barry were discredited.

effects of the quiz show scandal can still be felt in today's game show programming. The FBI insists that it has instituted so many safeguards that it would be almost impossible to fix a game show again.

The Rise of TV Talk Shows

Another popular programming format that got its start in the early 1950s is the evening talk show. The networks figured that a talk show format would be a pretty inexpensive way to lure the insomniacs away from the tired old rerun movies "The Late Show" was airing each night after the late news. They were right. Steve Allen made his debut as the host of NBC's "Tonight Show," in September 1954. Although popular and successful as a talk show host right from the start, Allen left the "Tonight Show" in 1957 to devote his energies to his own prime-time variety show. Jack Paar took his place and hosted the show until Johnny Carson took over in 1962. By then, NBC's "Tonight Show" had become a permanent programming fixture other networks tried hard to copy or dislodge.

Kids' Shows

Programming for kids appeared as early as 1947 with the "Howdy Doody Show," featuring the rebellious prankster, Clarabelle the clown. Other early children's favorites included the "Adventures of Rin Tin Tin," "Ding Dong School," the "Pinky Lee Show," "Rootie Kazootie," and a puppet show called "Kukla, Fran and Ollie." In 1955, Robert Keeshan,

who had previously played Clarabelle the clown, left NBC's "Howdy Doody Show" in a pay dispute and defected to CBS, who made him the star of a new show for preschool kids, "Captain Kangaroo." On this show, which won awards for actually putting the welfare of children ahead of the sponsor, unlike most of the fifties programming for kids, the Captain was joined by such characters as Mr. Greenjeans, Grandfather Clock, and Silly Billy.

Saturday morning cartoons like CBS's "Mighty Mouse Playhouse" were also aired for the first time in 1955. That same year, ABC also premiered its hour-long "Mickey Mouse Club" with host Jimmie Dodd. This program was produced by Walt Disney and featured everything from cartoons and short films to morality lectures by cartoon character Jiminy Cricket. The real stars, however, were the Mouseketeers, kid stars like Mickey Rooney, Jr., and Annette Funicello, who later became the teen star of the sixties beach blanket movies. No other children's program has ever been as successful as the "Mickey Mouse Club" in its short reign from 1955 to 1959. Fan mail for the show poured in at a rate of seventy-five hundred letters a month from enthusiastic kids all over the country.

But adult and children's entertainment was far from being the only noteworthy programming this new invention offered the American public. Just as important was the impact it had on communicating the news.

TV News Invents Itself

It was not an easy process. In the beginning, newscasts were complicat-

"[The producer] instructed me on how to answer the questions. . . . He gave me a script to memorize. . . . I would give almost anything I have to reverse the course of my life in the last three years."

Charles Van Doren, 1959

ed, with bulky filming equipment, weird props, ugly mikes, puppets, and even a chimpanzee. To begin with, the really good radio news broadcasters after World War II were pretty skeptical about the idea of television. They were puzzled at the thought that radio network producers wanted to include pictures in a news broadcast. Many thought the whole concept was straight out of science fiction and they were not about to risk their careers on a passing fad.

As a result, early television news programs were not able to lure the better existing news broadcasters away from radio. Instead, they recruited broadcasters from the ranks of local newspaper reporters. Walter Cronkite, a gutsy war correspondent and former Moscow bureau chief for the United Press, entered the broadcasting booth in 1950 as the first reporter assigned exclusively to television in CBS's Washington bureau. He went on to anchor CBS evening news for over twenty years.

In those days, television still consisted of newsreels and radio-style news reporting. Videotape, minicams, and three-way satellite hookups had not yet been invented, and there were no such things as computer graphics or instant replays. In fact, no one had ever used the word "anchorman," let alone "anchorwoman." The

Early TV relied on gimmicks to capture audience attention. Here "Buffalo" Bob Smith tries it all ways with a puppet called Howdy Doody and Zippy, a live chimp. The "Howdy Doody Show" was a popular afternoon babysitter from 1947, when it premiered, until 1960, when the curtain came down for the last time. After thirteen years and 2,343 episodes, Clarabelle the clown broke her silence with the parting words "Goodnight kids."

format of news shows was pretty unsophisticated in those early days, too. When NBC started its highly successful morning "Today Show," starring Dave Garroway, they teamed him up with an endearing chimpanzee costar named J. Fredd Muggs. Not to be outdone, CBS started its own morning news broadcast in the mid-1950s with Walter Cronkite playing straight man to a number of puppets, including one named Charlemagne the Lion. The Walter Cronkite-puppet combination didn't work, however, and they were eventually replaced by Jack Paar.

Network news really came of age in 1951, when the development of coaxial cable and microwave relays made it possible to broadcast from coast to coast. Before that, programs originating in New York could not even get as far west as Chicago. The CBS network was the first to dominate the evening news market with a program called "Douglas Edwards with the News." William S. Paley, who headed CBS at that time, put Edward R. Murrow in charge of recruiting some of the best reporters in the world, including William L. Shirer, Howard K. Smith, Robert Trout, Eric Sevareid, and Charles Collingwood. He wanted reporters who already knew how to go out and get a story and then present it with an intelligent analysis. It didn't take these reporters long to catch on to the video dimension.

Early News Competition

The early newscasts were pretty crude. After all, they had no invisible boom mikes, no off-screen teleprompters, no glitzy sets, and no hookups to live action in faraway places. The newscaster simply read the news directly from his written notes into a large, clumsy-looking microphone sitting in the middle of his desk. Then one of the directors got the idea to hang a clock behind the newscaster so the audience would get the idea that it was a live show, happening right before their eyes. Not to be outdone, a director on a competing network hung two clocks behind his news broadcaster, with the second clock showing the time on the West Coast — even though no one on the West Coast could watch New York television in 1951. Pretty soon, network news became a game of "can you top this?" When Douglas Edwards at CBS had three clocks and a calendar, then NBC's John Cameron Swayze had to have a map. Not to be outdone, Edwards' program then included a world globe. When Swayze added a black telephone to his desk paraphernalia, Edwards retaliated by adding in and out baskets and an executive pen set. Probably the only people who really cared about this silliness were the people in each of the network newsrooms, but this kind of network competition was typical in the early days of television.

Sponsors also played an important part in news programs right from the beginning. For example, the main news broadcaster for the now-defunct DuMont network, Mike Wallace, would deliver fifteen minutes of the nightly news and then walk over to a second set where he had to give an impassioned sales pitch for Bond suits. Bond was the Manhattan clothier sponsoring the program.

This kind of commercialism was by no means unusual in the early days of TV news. NBC's first nightly

newscast, "Camel News Caravan," was sponsored by Camel cigarettes. As part of the contract, the advertising agency insisted that an ever-lit Camel cigarette had to be burning in an ashtray located prominently at John Cameron Swayze's elbow, and the network had to make sure that every shot of Swayze also showed the pack of Camels lying casually on his desk. In many cases, the commercials stole the spotlight from the news coverage. When CBS covered the 1952 Republican convention, Westinghouse Electric sponsored the coverage. Day after day, the often boring coverage of the convention floor fights was interrupted by an attractive TV hostess named

Betty Furness, the spokesperson for Westinghouse, who discussed the finer points of ranges and refrigerators. The most popular commercial spokeswoman of the fifties, Furness became the model for the ideal 1950s housewife; many people kept watching the convention coverage just to see her.

TV news was not just fluff and silliness, however. As early as 1951, programs like CBS's "See It Now" set new standards of hard-hitting journalism for TV news. Noted for its thorough reporting and incisive editing, it broke new ground by moving from the studio to out on location. Its film cameras went everywhere, and the show rapidly developed a reputation for its willingness to tackle tough issues. The best example was its coverage of Joseph McCarthy and the army hearings on March 9, 1954. Edward R. Murrow and Fred Friendly hosted the news coverage that let Americans see for themselves how McCarthy bullied and outmaneuvered his opponents in his witch hunt for subversive Communists. Perhaps even more important, Murrow and Friendly provided editorial comment after the broadcast that finally helped Americans see McCarthy for who he really was. "This is no time for men who oppose his methods to keep silent," Murrow said at the end of one broadcast. "We can deny our heritage but we cannot escape responsibility for the result." Overwhelmingly, viewers agreed with him.

Other significant news coverage in the fifties that changed forever the way TV reporters would get their stories was CBS's exclusive interview in 1957 with Fidel Castro, two years before he violently overthrew Cuba's leader, Fulgencio Batista. To get the interview, CBS reporters had to hike up to Castro's secret Cuban mountain retreat (with 250 pounds of camera equipment) and follow him around for ten days. It was a tough assignment, but it was the only way that the Cuban revolutionary would agree to the interview.

This and other exclusive news stories kept the competition hot between the networks for news coverage. By the late 1950s, CBS and NBC had grown to about two hundred stations apiece, which meant that they had local people available to cover news that was happening live almost anywhere in the United States. News anchormen and reporters who got their starts in the TV news reporting of the fifties went on to dominate broadcast news for the next several decades — people like Murrow, Sevareid, Wallace, and, of course, the NBC coanchors Chet Huntley and David Brinkly, who became the most famous reporting duo in the history of television.

The Impact of Television

It's possible that Americans adapted so easily to the sudden changes television made in their lives because they desperately needed a mass diversion from the frightening politics of the Cold War and the nuclear arms race. Another reason for its increase in popularity was the new-found American affluence. Not only did early television offer new choices of entertainment, owning one increased one's status in the community. It also had a definite impact on other entertainment industries. After the initial set payments, TV in the fifties was virtually free. As a result, people went out less in the

> "We must not confuse dissent with disloyalty."
>
> Edward R. Murrow, 1953

evenings and devoted their spare time to watching the tube. Since watching TV was both cheaper than going out and involved less effort, the movie industry, theater, concerts, nightclubs, even sporting events suffered from the lack of attendance.

TV was also a more intrusive medium that radio ever was. A person could work on all sorts of different projects while listening to the radio, but a TV program demanded the attention of both eyes *and* ears. Producers understood right from the beginning that TV was most effective (and most interesting) when the message was simple and fast paced. That's why most TV commercials until now have been between thirty and sixty seconds long at most. This programming focus often tended to reduce life to easy-to-understand but overly simplistic concepts.

With television came the junk food craze. In 1950 alone, Americans consumed 750 million pounds of hot dogs and 320 million pounds of potato chips. Frozen TV dinners were an immediate hit, as were sets of folding TV trays. This allowed both Mom and the rest of the family to spend the maximum time in front of the TV. On one hand, American families were spending more time together in the evening than they ever had before. On the other hand, there was very little actual communication between these family members. They just all happened to be in the same room together, watching TV.

Even by the early fifties, television had become the prime source of entertainment for the nation's children. Parents who once couldn't coax their children into the house, suddenly found it impossible to pry them away from the TV set. These young viewers, suitably dressed for the occasion, are transfixed by "Hopalong Cassidy," in January 1950.

At first, television was hailed as a tool of universal communication, a medium that would provide all Americans with a broader, more democratic view of the world and its events. The fact that so many Americans were buying and watching television seemed to prove that America had become a truly classless and democratic society. It acted like a mirror, reflecting the wholesome, family-oriented, God-fearing, law-abiding, middle-class image Americans wanted so desperately to believe in. They thought it provided unbiased and uncensored information on the world around them. But as private firms and individuals scrambled to gain control of television programming, TV became more and more a tool of commercial and political manipulation. The creative and experimental programming of the golden age of television in the early fifties soon vanished. Its place was taken by a bland, pretaped, homogenized product.

Racist Roles for Minorities

One issue that TV programming did not even pretend to address fairly was race. There were very few minority performers on TV in the fifties, let alone nonwhite performers who had their own programs. Part of this was due to sponsors and network managers who were afraid that it would cause too much public controversy. African-American singer Bob Howard had a series called "Sing It Again" in the late forties, but it was cancelled shortly

Singer Nat "King" Cole was among the first African-Americans to star in his own successful TV show. By the end of 1956, Cole had sold more than twenty million records. Here, he teaches his seven-year-old daughter Sweetie how to sing and play the piano just like her pa.

after it made its debut. The first African-American to have his own long-running network television show in the fifties was popular singer Nat "King" Cole. He was featured for fifteen minutes each evening, accompanying his rich voice on the piano.

On the whole, though, if blacks and members of other American minority groups appeared on television at all, it was either in the role of comic prop (like Benny's manservant Rochester on "The Jack Benny Show") or, far more rarely, in special appearances in "Hallmark Hall of Fame" or other more highbrow dramas. In general, minorities were kept out of mainstream TV programming because they did not fit in with the image that television wished to present of America. Members of these minority groups appeared only in purely racist roles, such as savage, scalp-hunting Indians, wiggling Polynesian dancing girls, sleepy, shiftless Mexicans with sombreros and serapes, or crafty, inscrutable "Chinamen" like the wily Charlie Chan.

In the early fifties, the programming excellence created by great performers from Lucille Ball and Milton Berle to Edward R. Murrow and Walter Cronkite hinted at the tremendous potential of television to influence American culture. Unfortunately, that golden age was short lived. By the late fifties, the programming was firmly under the control of sponsors who insisted on banality and formula writing. Gone were the exciting days of live television, and in its place was the tinny, false sound of canned laughter, escalating violence, and mindless sitcoms.

Comedian Jack Benny was another successful TV import from radio. His jokes and familiar mannerisms, such as the shrug and raised eyebrow, made audiences roar. His stooge Eddie "Rochester" Anderson was the butt of many of his jokes and was typecast in the role of brainless black manservant.

CHAPTER 10
Rock 'n' Roll and So Much More

These teenagers are rocking in the aisles and on the seats of New York's Paramount Theatre during one of disk jockey Alan Freed's rock 'n' roll stage shows in 1957. Freed claimed to have coined the phrase "rock 'n' roll," and certainly did much to promote the music with live concerts and regular radio programs. For the young people of America, the loud music with its driving beat was a powerful and exciting escape from a mundane suburban existence.

Imagining the 1950s without rock 'n' roll is to visualize a construction site without noise. Yet, before the middle of the decade, there was very little rock, and the music itself went by several names. To middle-class parents, it might be called "boogie-woogie" or "race music," terms covering anything played or sung with vitality by African-Americans on a few big-city AM radio stations. To blacks themselves, it was known as R & B —

rhythm and blues. Religious blacks might recognize traces of gospel music. To rural, southern white people, it could be called country swing. And to northern vocalists, who substituted their voices for instruments, it was doo-wop. It went by almost as many names as it had origins.

Did real rock 'n' roll begin when a teenage Baltimore songwriter named Deborah Chessler hooked up with vocalists Sonny Til and the Orioles in

the early fifties to produce a string of modest hits? Did it start when Little Richard, a young black man from Georgia, sent a tape to Specialty Records in 1954? Perhaps rock didn't begin until "white boys started singing black boys' music" — in which case Mississippi's Elvis Presley and Louisiana's Jerry Lee Lewis should share the honors. Beginnings don't matter; what matters is rock's effect on the fifties and the decades to follow.

Can't Keep a Good Thing Down

Rock music captured the hearts of millions of young people in 1954 and 1955, with hits from Bill Haley and the Comets such as "Shake, Rat-tle and Roll" and "Rock Around the Clock." Haley was a Texan, his band a bunch of country musicians in plaid tuxedoes, and they excelled at delivering their own songs and cleaned-up versions of tunes heard in black roadhouses. Elvis, Lewis, Little Richard, Johnny Ace, Johnny Otis, and groups such as Hank Ballard and the Midnighters, the Platters, Clyde McPhatter and the Drifters, and Billy Ward and the Dominoes produced music that was simply too vibrant to keep off the airwaves. White-owned radio stations — and almost all were white owned — tried to satisfy teens with wimpy rock ballads, such as Eddie Fisher's "Dungaree Doll" or Kay Starr's "Rock and Roll Waltz." But the kids knew the difference. Overnight, rock was everywhere.

Bill Haley and the Comets leapt to number one in the music charts in May 1955 with "Rock Around the Clock," following the runaway success of their movie The Blackboard Jungle, *which included the hit song. Haley's blend of rhythm and blues with a country swing shook teenagers out of their apathy. Boston religious leaders urged the banning of rock 'n' roll and a Connecticut psychiatrist called rock a "communicable disease." But, to the delight of most American teenagers, the rock 'n' roll era had begun.*

Harry Belafonte, with his wonderful liquid voice, was more to adult tastes than the raw energy of rock 'n' roll. Crooners like Belafonte, Sinatra, and Tony Bennett would enjoy excellent album sales in a decade when the likes of Elvis, the Drifters, and Little Richard dominated the jukebox and sales of forty-five rpm records.

The reasons for rock 'n' roll's success were as varied as its sources. Former radio station listeners turned to television for their entertainment, so stations owners were forced by the popularity of television to find a new audience. Radio spread the word, since rock concerts were few and far between and were held in theaters seating only a few hundred. There weren't many huge arenas at the time, and places like the Hollywood Bowl or New York City's Carnegie Hall were devoted to classical or jazz music. And since the audience was so young (the baby boom began in 1946, which would make the first boomers only nine years of age in 1955), a fun thing to do was to tune in the radio. Young listeners also bought millions of forty-five rpm (revolutions per minute) records, which contained one song on each side for less than a dollar.

Because young people did not have limitless funds, long-playing (LP) records, which played at 331/3 rpm and contained about a dozen songs, continued to cater to adult tastes. Names like Frank Sinatra, Harry Belafonte, and Henry Mancini dominated album sales. The popularity of albums continued into the late 1950s, when stereo records and phonographs were widely available. Seventy-eight rpm records continued to be popular with rhythm and blues audiences and were produced until 1959. They were larger and heavier than the forty-five records, though they, too, only contained one song per side because of the speed at which the big record spun beneath the needle.

Frank Sinatra.

No entertainer in American history has been more successful than "Ol' Blue Eyes," Frank Sinatra. Born into a musically talented Italian-American family in Hoboken, New Jersey, across the Hudson River from New York City, Sinatra has sounded so good for so long that *Rolling Stone* magazine once claimed, "The voice has a life of its own."

That voice first gained national attention during World War II, as bobbysoxers (teenage girls) screamed and swooned when the crooner sang, usually accompanied by a snappy orchestra with a dozen or more instruments. Though thin and rather sharp-featured, Sinatra was soon signed by Hollywood to appear in films. He made several lightweight hits, ranging from *Anchors Aweigh* (1945) to *High Society* (1956). In the latter film, he was teamed with fellow entertainment immortals Bing Crosby and Louis Armstrong.

But it was his success as a dramatic actor that surprised and pleased fans and critics. Beginning in 1953 in *From Here to Eternity,* and continuing in such films as *The Naked Runner* in 1967, Sinatra showed a firm grasp of a variety of characters and was a big box-office draw. All the while he was singing — on radio, on television, and in personal appearances everywhere, but especially in Las Vegas.

Sinatra helped put Las Vegas on the map. Located some two hundred miles east of Los Angeles, the small city legalized gambling and hoped for the best after World War II. Visitors were treated to performances by Sinatra and others, who were paid handsome sums from money earned by casinos. Sinatra and organized-crime bosses have been linked, stemming from life in Las Vegas in the 1950s, but nothing has ever been proven. Originally a Democrat, the entertainer was snubbed by the Kennedys prior to the 1960 election and has been a Republican ever since. He was even linked romantically with Nancy Reagan — during her husband's presidency!

Through it all, the voice has become a bit strained, but it just keeps going. Songs such as "My Way," exuding warmth and a hint of menace, probably will be playing long after this star of the 1950s — and surrounding decades — is show business history.

Alan Freed and Dick Clark

Perhaps the first rock concert took place in Cleveland in 1952. An overwhelmingly African-American audience was treated to a number of bands introduced by Alan Freed, a local disk jockey known by his radio name, Moondog. Freed left Cleveland's WJW in 1954, hired to put radio station WINS in New York City on the map. He certainly did that, as well as promote live performances and even play the part of a rock promoter in a

Hollywood movie. But the man who claimed to have first called the new music rock 'n' roll became involved in payola — accepting money from record companies to play their songs and publicize their artists. Freed was fired by WABC radio in New York in 1959 and eventually received a suspended sentence for bribery. He died in 1965 at the age of forty-two.

Even more popular than Freed was Dick Clark, a clean-cut youngster from upstate New York who served as host on "American Bandstand," a teenage dance show that originated in Philadelphia and was soon broadcast daily on the ABC television network. Clark's squeaky-clean appearance and

his insistence that the young dancers dress well made rock 'n' roll seem almost respectable. Growing young girls set aside their Betsy Wetsy dolls and young boys their Revell model-battleship kits to watch the dancing, see guest performers, and to look at the kids from Philly rate the new tunes. Clark was called before Congress in 1960 about payola, but it did nothing to harm his career.

Rock 'n' roll was an easy thing to attack in an election year. Lyrics were sometimes suggestive, the driving beat reminded some listeners of sex itself, the music allowed blacks and whites to mix easily, and the whole scene was something adults simply did not

By the middle of the decade, rock 'n' roll was everywhere. The church hated it; parents, psychologists, and educators were troubled by it. But teenagers, like this 1956 couple, just couldn't get enough.

Little Richard was always one of the best at combining those magic rock 'n' roll ingredients: great showmanship plus a fast and furious style of playing — in Little Richard's case, the piano. His "Lucille" was a huge hit in 1957.

understand. That made the music all the more desirable to teenagers, though radio stations often refused to play tunes disliked by station management. In the South, songs by blacks sometimes had to be sung by whites in order to be broadcast. Singers such as Pat Boone made a small fortune delivering their own versions of tunes that originated with Fats Domino, Little Richard, and others. Institutions such as bandleader Mitch Miller and the Roman Catholic Church attacked rock for its lyrics and for its apparent evil, but that only served to increase its attraction.

Delivering a hit record wasn't all that difficult. In 1957, a bunch of young white guys calling themselves The Diamonds made an exaggerated demo of a song by a bunch of black guys who called themselves The Gladiolas. The song, "Little Darlin'," zoomed to the top of the charts and stayed there for months. Every radio station and record store worthy of the name issued weekly lists of popular records. Radio stations made big deals out of "The Weekly Countdown," wherein the top thirty or forty or even fifty records in the country would be played, beginning with the newest or

"[Rock 'n' Roll could] induce medieval types of spontaneous lunacy [even] prehistoric rhythmic trances."

A psychologist, after attending one of Alan Freed's musical extravaganzas

Jerry Lee Lewis dances on top of his piano as competently as his flying fingers can play it. "Whole Lot of Shaking Going On" was one of his greatest hits in 1957.

least popular and eventually arriving at number one. Kids simply could not get enough.

The Downside of Rock

Everybody even remotely connected with the music was getting rich, but the money came at a price. Traveling from one nightly engagement to the next, rockers such as Buddy Holly, the Big Bopper, and Mexican-American sensation Ritchie Valens died in plane crashes. Or, like West Coast vocalist Eddie Cochran, they died in car crashes. Drugs had not yet cut a path through the music business, but there were other risks involved. Legendary black rocker Chuck Berry spent time in prison for failing to pay taxes and for transporting a fourteen-year-old girl across a state line. Piano pumper Jerry Lee Lewis was blackballed because he married his thirteen-year-old second cousin.

Equally frustrating, not many performers made much money from their records. They depended instead on live performances, where they frequently received a percentage of all the tickets sold.

Elvis Presley, the Tupelo Trucker

One who did profit from his singing career, of course, was Elvis Presley. A teenage truck driver from Tupelo, Mississippi, Elvis recorded a tune for his mother's birthday and within a year or two was the best known singer on Earth. Presley appeared on television frequently in the mid-1950s, though his hip wiggling was considered obscene and he was shown only from the guitar up.

"The King," as he enjoyed being called, had a good, if untrained voice, and he put together a string of hits that did not stop for almost a decade. Presley also enjoyed a solid movie career. Beginning in 1956 with *Love Me Tender*, Elvis made more than a dozen movies, most of which were used to feature him performing his songs.

Elvis was everywhere. In 1956, for example, his songs were rated number one in *Billboard* magazine for twenty-five weeks of the year. His 1956 record royalties exceeded $6 million. Presley performed a year

Elvis Presley. (1935-1977)

Elvis Presley was the first and the most legendary American rock 'n' roll star. He could not have achieved that crown without television, which not only delivered his songs into U.S. living rooms but his handsome and hip-wriggling self, as well.

Presley was a poor white boy from Tupelo, Mississippi. He graduated from high school and took a job as a truck driver, all the while playing the guitar and singing his own versions of bluesy, black roadhouse tunes. He recorded his first commercial record in 1954 and, under the guidance of manager Colonel Tom Parker, obtained a recording contract with RCA two years later. Equally important, Parker was able to book Presley on "The Ed Sullivan Show," a popular, hour-long variety program that aired on the CBS television network every Sunday evening.

The singer caused a sensation by gyrating his hips and generally exuding sexuality as he sang. Because of his conduct, the cameras were allowed to train on him only from the waist up. Despite the brief censorship, "Elvis the Pelvis" became a favorite of young men and women all across the land; his likeness and his voice were everywhere. Not even brief service in the U.S. Army could diminish his popularity, which continued into the early 1960s.

Popular Presley tunes included "All Shook Up," "Don't Be Cruel," "Heartbreak Hotel," "Hound Dog," "Jailhouse Rock," and "Love Me Tender." He made a number of movies, most of them built around his songs, such as *Viva Las Vegas* (1963), *Paradise Hawaiian Style* (1966), and many more. His brand of rock music was an expression of fifties youthful rebellion.

Unfortunately, Presley failed to keep up with current musical trends. When the Beatles, the Rolling Stones, and other British acts invaded the U.S., and when psychedelic music took over the pop music charts and FM radio stations, Presley became less visible. In fact, he disliked many of the newer performers. He gained weight and became more of an establishment, Las Vegas-style lounge act than a rebellious singer of bold music.

Presley had a sprawling mansion in Memphis and all the money, cars, toys, jewelry, jumpsuits, and bodyguards he could ever want. Yet he became morose, reliant on drugs prescribed by a physician friend. Like many younger rockers, Elvis overdosed, dying at the age of forty-two in one of his many bathrooms. His home, Graceland, and his records continue to be popular to this day.

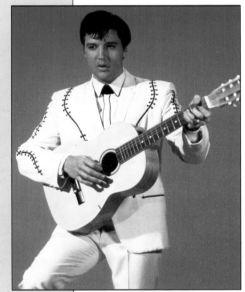

"Ah act the way ah feel."

Elvis Presley, 1955

earlier before a theater filled with screaming girls in Jacksonville, Florida, and several young women stormed the stage in an attempt to remove his clothes. He influenced young men, too. Guitar sales went from 228,000 in 1950 to 300,000 in 1955 to 400,000 in 1959. Boys tried to grow sideburns and, failing that, they combed their hair into the kind of slick cone seen atop Presley's young head.

Seeing the Stars

Rock movies were popular with the young. For kids who might live in the middle of nowhere without TV, it was their only chance to see the great performers belt out their tunes. Fats Domino, Jerry Lee Lewis, Little Richard, and many lesser-known celebrities appeared in rockin' low-budget movies such as *The Girl Can't Help It* and *High School Confidential*. For those with a Philco, Crosely, or RCA television set, the stars came out for half an hour every Saturday evening on "Dick Clark's American Bandstand," which featured live performances by current hitmakers beginning in 1957.

The music was assaulted by parents and lawmakers, and the musicians seemed unusually self-destructive. It frightened Little Richard so badly that the man with the piercing voice and the thundering piano feared he would go to hell, so he quit the business in 1958 to preach (though he would return later on).

The deaths, the crowds, the excitement, and the probability that people were being paid to play certain records caused a momentary vacuum in the business by the end of the decade. Even Elvis Presley was silent, having been inducted into the U.S. Army for a two-year hitch beginning in 1959 and winding up in West Germany. The vacuum was filled by Frankie Avalon, Fabian, Ricky Nelson, and Annette Funicello, good-looking young people of questionable talent who were packaged and sold as teen idols over the air, on TV, and in the movies.

Folk, Pop, and Jazz

There were, of course, other kinds of music. A clean-cut threesome calling themselves the Kingston Trio began performing at a club named the

Fats Domino's bluesy vocal style and rolling rhythms introduced a more laid back style to the pop music stable and helped popularize rhythm and blues. Two of his biggest hits were "Ain't It a Shame," in 1955 and "Blueberry Hill," in 1957.

Hungry i in San Francisco. They sang folk ballads, accompanied only by their own acoustic guitars or by an occasional banjo. Their shows were small and intimate, and they seemed more authentic and intellectual than any rocker you'd care to name. Other folksingers at the time included the Weavers, led by longtime folksinger Pete Seeger, and such antiestablishment types as Dave Van Ronk. Folk music was heard most often on college radio stations, though it would be a real force with a larger audience in the decade to come.

A driving force for folk music — and rock 'n' roll — was a young man named Robert Zimmerman. He grad-

uated from high school in Hibbing, Minnesota, in 1959 after having run away from home at least six times. He enrolled at the University of Minnesota that fall, but spent more time in coffee houses playing his acoustic guitar than he did in the classroom. A fan of traditional folk music but with an ear for rock, the man who would change his name to Bob Dylan took off for a livelier folk scene — Greenwich Village in New York City, the East Coast anchor of the 1950s beatnik scene. Within two years, the singer signed a contract with Columbia Records and made a hit album. Several years after that, Dylan would deeply influence the Beatles, the British group that

By the end of the decade, another musical alternative was coming to the fore: Folk singing threw off its pedestrian yoke and became protest music. Bob Dylan was soon to become the master at expressing pent-up rage, fear, and disappointment, as well as love and tenderness. Inspired initially by Pete Seeger, Dylan quickly established his own distinctive style, which was to develop in later years into a powerful mix of folk and rock.

would become the 1960s biggest rock act.

Another folk singer who would have an impact was Joan Baez. Of Hispanic heritage, Baez and her bell-like voice wowed the crowd at the Newport (Rhode Island) Folk Festival in 1959. A California native who grew up in Boston, she could count stars such as Harry Belafonte among her fans. Two other women who left indelible marks on music were Billie Holiday, nicknamed "Lady Day," and Carol King. Holiday's cool voice flowed out of Harlem clubs and into the hearts of black and white audiences alike. Brooklyn-born King wrote dozens of hits, from "Up on the Roof" performed by the Drifters to "Loco-Motion" sung by Little Eva. She would become a star in her own right, but not until the 1970s.

Singers with their own television shows at various times included Perry Como, Frank Sinatra, and Andy Williams. Every variety show, from Ed Sullivan's "Toast of the Town" to "The Jackie Gleason Show" featured at least one musical act, though it was more likely to be one or a group of rockers as the decade progressed. Local imitations of "American Bandstand" were seen on Saturday or Sunday afternoons on TVs all across the country.

If folk and pop won general approval, jazz still was seen as slightly shady, though there certainly were great jazz musicians during the 1950s. They included a succession of wonderful pianists, including Cy Walter, Bill Clifton, Earl Wilde, Errol Garner, Oscar Peterson, and George Shearing. But there were other jazz artists, many of them horn players such as Dizzy Gillespie or Miles Davis. Dave Brubeck, leader of a quartet, was virtually a household name with recordings such as "Take Five." *Playboy* magazine's annual poll of favorite musicians was overwhelmingly devoted to jazz from its inception in 1953. Small clubs in urban areas played host to a range of black and white jazz greats.

Berry Gordy, Jr., and Motown

Just as the decade was ending, a black Detroit autoworker who was earning $90 a week at the Ford Motor Company made a big decision. Berry Gordy, Jr., realized that the songs he wrote in his spare time were popular locally and wondered if he could make a living off the tight rhymes and smooth phrases. Gordy borrowed $700 and started Gordy Records. His first song, without benefit of national distribution, sold sixty thousand copies. From that first sale Gordy created two other record labels, Tamla and Motown. He penned a song, "Shop Around," for a group known as Smokey Robinson and the Miracles, and by the end of 1960, Gordy had his first gold record, "Please Mr. Postman," by a female group known as the Marvelettes. By 1967, annual Motown sales reached $30 million! In an era when African-Americans were shut out of the business end of recording, Berry Gordy, Jr., proved that talent was colorblind.

Bo Diddley, Gary "U.S." Bonds, Mickey and Sylvia, Professor Longhair, Link Wray and the Ray-Men, and hundreds of others on long-gone labels such as Sun, Speciality, Liberty, Stax and Chess, were played until the grooves became scratched and the records had to be replaced.

CHAPTER 11
Ten Impressive Years of Sports

Before the military service was fully integrated, before all public schools saw a mix of black and white students, before interstate transportation was open equally to everyone, amateur and professional sports in the United States were racially mixed. The last major sport to be integrated was "the national pastime" — baseball. Jackie Robinson joined the Brooklyn Dodgers in 1947, opening the way not only for fellow African-Americans but for players from the Caribbean and Latin America, where baseball was very popular.

To succeed, Robinson had to be better than most. A college football star at UCLA and a U.S. Army officer in World War II, he earned Rookie of the Year honors and went on to play for the Dodgers for a decade. A second baseman, Robinson was named Most Valuable Player in the National League in 1949 when he batted .342 — he got on base more than once for every three times at bat. Many opponents were white southern athletes eager to bait or even injure the lone black man. But Robinson was followed by Larry Doby with the American League Cleveland Indians, and then by scores of players from all ethnic backgrounds. Baseball became more popular than ever.

A visit to the Baseball Hall of Fame in Cooperstown, New York, indicates that great minority players were waiting for a chance to swing their bats in the big leagues. They included African-Americans such as the Dodgers' Roy Campanella, the Braves' Henry Aaron, and the Reds' Frank Robinson. Hispanic players included Roberto Clemente of the Pirates, Juan Marichal of the Giants, and Luis Aparicio of the White Sox. While women were banned from competing in major league baseball by team owners in 1952, from 1943 to 1954 there was an All-American Girls Professional Baseball League.

Why Baseball Was Big League

What made big league baseball "big?" It was divided into two leagues with permanent home fields in major cities. Every team had a network of radio stations that broadcast games over a wide area, and newspaper and magazine coverage of the games was generous, constant, and not all that critical. Very few players were well paid; most had to take off-season jobs to make ends meet. This pay equity between player and fan helped shape baseball's popularity. Minor league teams in smaller cities were places where very young players, often right out of high school, honed their skills. They, too, were poorly paid but endured the long seasons (as many as 154 games over six months) for a chance at athletic stardom. No city worthy of the name was without its own major or minor league team. The

"Don't look back. Something may be gaining on you."

Baseball star
Satchel (Leroy) Paige

"Nice guys finish last."

Baseball manager
Leo Durocher

World Series, pitting the best National League team against the best American League team each October, could last as long as seven games and was the country's most followed sports event.

The last big league team to integrate its roster was the Boston Red Sox in 1959. By that time, African-American players such as Ernie Banks and Willie Mays were the game's superstars. They and other white players made small sums of money endorsing cigarettes or by using certain brands of baseball gloves or bats. No professional athlete made nearly as much money endorsing as he or she did participating, though professional golfers did very well with bags, balls, clubs, and clothing. But once television began to cover games, owner revenues climbed and so eventually did the players' salaries.

Though most high schools had boys' baseball teams, baseball wasn't a big deal in most schools. Rather, it was organized in the summer in the form of Little League (players under the age of twelve), Pony League (young teens), and teams sponsored by organizations such as the American Legion and others for older teenage players. Girls played softball in leagues, as did adults, most of them males, however. The boys' various leagues offered a kid a big league type uniform, a small field where the average

The Brooklyn Dodgers battle it out against the New York Yankees at Ebbets Field, in the baseball World Series of 1956. The Yankees finally won the series by four games to the Dodgers three.

boy might be able to hit a home run, and parental involvement. Little League parks were a common place to find Mom and Dad on Saturday or Sunday afternoons. While Dad coached or encouraged from the bleachers, Mom sold soft drinks and popcorn to raise money for seasons to come.

Football

Football, played without face guards in the 1950s, was popular at high schools all over the country. Friday nights in the fall would find hundreds of local residents at the school ballfield to see the high school team take on an out-of-town rival. Following high school, talented players with

adequate grades could receive scholarships to play the game at colleges large and small. College football, thanks to television, became more popular as the decade progressed. Several bowl games, broadcast on New Year's Day over network TV, offered easy viewing after a New Year's Eve party.

Colleges outside the South displayed integrated football teams in the 1950s, and National Football League teams ended a ban on African-Americans in 1946. Despite integration, there were lingering stereotypes. For example, no black athlete started regularly at quarterback until the 1970s!

Unlike in professional baseball, no one was nationally known before television. Pro football telecast well, and the rules were fine-tuned to make it

> *"Whoever wants to know the heart and mind of America had better learn baseball, the rules and realities of the game — and do it by watching first some high school or small-town teams."*
>
> Author Jacques Barzun

Jim Brown.

A member of the professional Football Hall of Fame, Jim Brown has been called by some observers the greatest offensive back in the history of American football. He may also have been the best all-around American athlete since Jim Thorpe. In fact, Brown was named Football Back of the Decade in the 1950s.

Born in Georgia, Brown moved with his family while a child to Long Island, New York. There, he learned to play many sports, all of them very well. By the time he was in high school, he was a star in baseball, basketball, football, lacrosse, and track and field. Dozens of colleges tried to recruit him, and he was given offers from two major league baseball teams, the New York Yankees and the Boston Braves.

Brown attended Syracuse University in upstate New York. He earned All-American honors in football and lacrosse, turning down offers in 1956 to participate in the decathlon (part of the Olympic Games), as well as a contract totaling $150,000 to become a professional boxer.

After college, Brown was drafted by the Cleveland Browns and immediately became their starting fullback. He led the league in rushing as a rookie and was part of a Cleveland team that won its division championship. His selection as Rookie of the Year was unanimous. He played for nine more years, scoring a total of 106 touchdowns and gaining 12,312 yards. Always in superb condition, he was seldom injured.

Brown retired from football while still a young man. He soon set about improving the lives of black businesspeople. His rugged good looks earned him numerous movie roles, usually in adventure films such as *Rio Conchos*, *The Dirty Dozen*, *Ice Station Zebra*, and *The Riot*. Living comfortably in California, he also founded the Negro Industrial and Economic Union, a group that arranges financing for black entrepreneurs.

Golf was good TV viewing. It was slow enough for anyone to follow and could enable armchair golfers to sit back and watch how it should be done. African-American were excluded from most clubs and major tournaments until the turn of the decade. Charles Sifford of Los Angeles was one of the first black golfers to be allowed into a pro-amateur tourney.

even more appealing to a living room filled with sports fans. Stars of the 1950s included Jim Brown, an African-American who played for the Cleveland Browns; Frank Gifford of the New York Giants, who is now a sportscaster; and Sammy Baugh of the Washington Redskins.

Basketball

The National Basketball Association became integrated in 1950 by Sweetwater Clifton, Chuck Cooper, and Earl Lloyd. The last team to hire a black player was the St. Louis Hawks in 1959. Between those two dates, African-American players gave strong hints that they would dominate the game in the future. The game's first black superstar was Elgin Baylor, who played for the Los Angeles Lakers. Other early stars, black and white, were Wilt Chamberlain, Bob Cousy, George Mikan, Oscar Robertson, and Dolph Schayes. The 1950s stars earned their keep, playing grueling schedules night after night for adequate but not huge salaries. Television patiently stayed with the game as it matured. Today, professional basketball's superstars are the most familiar names in American sports.

Basketball was played in virtually every college and high school. Women seldom competed against girls from other schools, but the high school Girls Athletic Associations were often centered around basketball. The game played by women at the time usually was half court — someone believed girls might collapse if required to run the length of a gym floor. There were six players to a side, and extensive dribbling was against the rules. Despite such handicaps, high school girls enjoyed the game, and it was especially popular in the state of Iowa. Boys' basketball was most popular in Indiana and in inner cities along the East Coast.

Other Professional Sports

Golf televised well and hockey didn't. Golf was slow and easy to follow, while hockey teams spread themselves all over the rink in complex, lightning formations. The puck moved at blinding speeds, whereas

golf balls rolled across greens at a pace any camera operator could follow. Equally important, golf could be attempted by anyone, whereas only the young and the fit strapped on skates and took to the ice. Consequently, professional hockey was confined to a few big U.S. and Canadian cities, and golf was everywhere. The pasture game became so popular that it was widely assumed a person could not succeed in business without knowing how to play. Golf courses were public or private; most excluded blacks and confined women to playing once a week on Ladies' Day.

Other professional sports with large followings included horseracing, boxing, and tennis. Horseracing was popular primarily because it was one of the few legal-gambling outlets available. When underdog Dark Street

Sugar Ray Robinson won the world middleweight title for the fourth time in 1957. Together with heavyweight Rocky Marciano, he remained popular among fans during the fifties, although general interest in the sport had waned.

beat the famed Native Dancer in 1953 in the Kentucky Derby, millions listened in or watched the race on TV. Boxing slumped in the fifties due to the number of shady characters associated with it, though heavyweight champ Rocky Marciano was wildly popular and above suspicion. Tennis featured Althea Gibson, the first African-American to play in the U.S. Lawn Tennis Nationals at Forest Hills in New York. Gibson was a star throughout the decade, winning Wimbledon in 1958. Maureen "Little Mo" Connolly, a smiling Californian, won pro tennis's three major tournaments in 1953.

Amateur Sports

The most stunning accomplishment of the 1950s took place in England in 1954. Roger Bannister, a lanky distance runner, became the first person to run a mile in less than four minutes. Bannister covered the mile in 3:59.4, becoming an instant, world-

U.S. tennis star Althea Gibson battles it out with Miss S. Reynolds of South Africa to defeat her 6-3, 6-4, in the Wimbledon Lawn Tennis Championships of 1957. Gibson was the first African-American to win the All-England title, just seven years after becoming the first player to break the color line when she played at Forest Hills.

Maureen Connolly. (1934-1969)

California produces talented athletes, primarily because the warm weather allows them to practice their sport every month of the year. Maureen Connolly took advantage of the year-round sun to become one of the best tennis players America ever produced.

Born and reared in San Diego, she began tennis lessons at the age of ten. Her coach discouraged left-handed play, so she switched and began to impress tennis experts with her skill. She practiced three hours a day, five days a week, winning a fifteen-and-under tournament at the age of eleven. In high school, she began to take tournament tennis seriously.

Named to the Wightman Cup team in the annual America-versus-Britain competition while a high school senior, she managed to defeat a twenty-nine-year-old British player. The following year, 1951, she won the nationals in Forest Hills, New York. She continued to win here and abroad until a fall from a horse prematurely ended competitive tennis for her in 1954.

Small by today's standards, "Little Mo" used rackets with custom handles designed for her small hands. Yet she showed a strong and consistent forehand shot that was proof of the hours of practice in sunny San Diego. Connolly, who died prematurely in 1969, was one of very few women to emerge from the 1950s as a well-known and popular athlete.

wide celebrity. In the Olympics, America's Bob Mathias became the only man to win the decathlon (a single event made up of various speed, skill, and strength contests) twice, in 1948 and 1952. Mathias's 1952 accomplishment overshadowed that of Cy Young, who became the first American ever to win the javelin throw. American men dominated track and field in the 1950s, with medals in other sports for men and women spread widely around. The Olympics were followed with increasing interest by American sports fans during the decade because several Soviet athletes did well enough to worry the United States.

To the average American, his or her favorite sports might have been bicycling, bowling, fishing, swimming, sledding, ice-skating, golf, or softball. Hardly a neighborhood existed that did not have at least a small area set aside for recreation. That area might include a paved portion with a hoop

for basketball, a baseball diamond, picnicking facilities, and a hill for winter sledding. Americans had more leisure time in the fifties, and they were looking for ways to spend it, whether playing back yard croquet while holding an ice-cold drink or heading "up north" to a fishing resort for a week or two of vacation every summer.

(Below) U.S. athlete Bob Mathias clears 3.90 meters during the decathlon pole-vault event at the Helsinki Olympics of 1952. He went on to win the gold, sharing that highest athletic honor with fellow Americans Lindig Rimingo (100 meters), and Andy Stanfield (200 meters), among others.

CHAPTER 12
Out of the Forties, into the Sixties

Throughout the fifties, the U.S. was involved in covert (secret) actions around the world, bolstering its anticommunist allies. One such ally was Reza Pahlavi, the shah of Iran. After five days of exile in Rome, the shah here reads a telegram confirming that the coup in his country has been crushed and that he should return to Tehran immediately. The United States assisted in overthrowing the popular coup leader, Dr. Mohammed Mossadegh, but would later regret its intervention in Iran.

America was a very different place by 1960 than it had been in 1950. As the decade began, those leaders running the country were people with strong memories of Great Depression hardships and of World War II. They had developed a mortal fear of communism, which was to lead them into a war on the remote Korean peninsula, and at home would generate a deep suspicion, bordering on paranoia, of any fellow American who dared think or act unconventionally. Since all Communists were atheists, they reasoned, all atheists were Communists. Thus it became necessary to embrace

Christianity in a very public manner if you were to avoid suspicion — if you didn't go to church on Sunday, you made sure you weren't seen until noon that day so that at least everyone thought you did. America became introverted and self-examining. After the horrors of Korea, the U.S. chose not to involve itself directly in world events such as the French war in Southeast Asia (1946-1954), although the U.S did send $60 million to aid the French in 1953. Nor did it send troops to help its World War II allies in their struggle for control over the Suez Canal in

1956. The U.S. provided arms to those it considered its friends — especially if they were fighting communists. It also engaged in covert activity around the world, overthrowing unfriendly governments and replacing them with administrations more to America's liking.

Barbarous Allies

The overall assignment of the CIA in the fifties was to stop communism, which they saw creeping like a cancer across the globe. To do this they had to manipulate people in many countries, often allying themselves with ignorant, murderous, or barbarous individuals, people with little or no regard for democracy.

One such dicator was Reza Pahlavi, the shah of Iran. He smothered political opposition in his country while pushing through huge pro-western economic and social changes. Dissent of any kind was stifled. The U.S. aided him in overthrowing the popular radical Dr. Mohammed Mossadegh, a move that it would regret in 1979, when the shah was overthrown and Iranian Islamic fundamentalists took over the U.S. Embassy in Tehran.

A Reevaluation

By the end of the fifties, Americans had been living for more than a decade under the threat of nuclear war. They had survived, and as some of the fear evaporated with familiarity, they were willing to let their leaders use atomic weapons as a tool of diplomacy. They tried to forget the threat that they could do nothing about and instead flung themselves into having families and settling into middle-class suburban society. By the end of the decade, however, cracks were beginning to appear in the veneer of suburban conformity. Blacks began agitating for their rights, inner-city decay was growing worse by the day, and women were growing bored with their stay-at-home existence. The nation's young were being "corrupted" by rock 'n' roll, and the Beat Generation was ques-

In a foretaste of what was to follow in the next decade, young members of the fifties Beat Generation rebelled against conformity and the monotony of suburban living. This couple at a 1950s dance with their loose, bohemian style of dress, were typical.

When a group of African-American students from North Carolina A & T College were refused service at a lunch counter in Woolworth's, Greensboro, they staged a sit-down strike. Ronald Martin (left), Robert Patterson (center), and Mark Martin (right) stayed seated at the counter all day. This was another form of nonviolent protest against segregation that characterized the civil rights movement in the late fifties and early sixties.

tioning the very moral fabric of the nation. The Beats, with their folk songs, their poems, and long evenings spent putting the world to rights over a bottle of wine — or two, mostly hung out with their friends in places such as San Francisco and Greenwich Village, in New York City. By the start of the new decade, there were enough of them to warrant their own newspaper. The *Village Voice* became the country's first alternative source for news, along with a magazine steeped in poor taste and produced by Paul Krassner, called the *Realist. On the Road,* by Jack Kerouac, epitomized the footloose restlessness of the beats. Beat or buttoned-down, black or white, college-bound or headed for the assembly-line, young people

in their millions began to question basic adult assumptions — and to look for alternatives.

If the fifties didn't quite change the world for the United States, it certainly paved the way for a big shake-up in the sixties. Out of the Beat Beneration the "Flower Generation" was born, preferring to drop out of American society altogether.

Paving the Way

By the end of the fifties, the Montgomery bus boycott and lunch counter sit-ins had drawn the nation's attention to the sorry plight of African-Americans. The passage of the Civil Rights Act of 1957 was to

set the country on the path towards ending segregation and extending civil rights to all Americans.

Meanwhile, the shock of the Soviet *Sputnik* space flight had jolted America's scientific community into expanding its space program. So much so that within eleven years of the first U.S. space launch, two Americans would set foot on the Moon's surface.

Declining Confidence

By the end of the decade, Americans began to suffer a crisis of confidence. They were aware of an education gap, a missile gap (real or imagined), increased crime, and slums. Economic growth had sputtered and stopped, there was growing apathy among the young, there was poverty, there was hate, and there was igno-

rance. Magazines and newspapers editorialized about whether the nation had a sense of purpose and what that purpose might be. There was the constant threat of the Cold War, yet few people believed that the proper response to the Soviets was the use of all-out nuclear weaponry. What was to be done?

Dwight Eisenhower himself was worried. He created a President's Commission on National Goals in February 1960 to tell him where the country was headed and which direction was the correct one. The ensuing report was so negative and so critical of the lack of action by the Eisenhower administration that Ike did not let the information out until well after the 1960 presidential election. But by that time, at least for the Republicans, it was too late. John F. Kennedy was president, and the 1960s, for better or worse, were under way.

Soviet premier Nikita Khrushchev says a few words on arrival at Andrews Air Force Base in September 1959, at the start of a twelve-day tour of the United States. On the platform with him are (from right to left): President Eisenhower; Secretary of State Christian Herter; Soviet Ambassador Mikhail Menshikov; Henry Cabot Lodge, U.S. Ambassador to the UN; and an interpreter. The rest are unidentified. During an earlier visit to Moscow by Richard Nixon, Khrushchev had accused the vice president of not knowing "anything about communism but fear of it."

KEY DATES

1950

January 14 —The U.S. recalls its consular officials from China after the Chinese seize the American consulate general in Peking.

January 31 — President Harry S Truman approves production of the hydrogen bomb.

June 25 — The United Nations asks its members for troops to help restore order in Korea.

June 27 — President Truman sends air force and navy personnel to Korea after the north invades the south. Ground forces are ordered to Korea three days later.

September 15 — U.S. forces land at Inchon, Korea, joining U.N. troops heading into northern Korea.

November 1 — Two members of a Puerto Rican nationalist movement try unsuccessfully to assassinate President Truman.

November 26 — Chinese troops cross the China-Korea border and attack UN forces.

1951

February 28 — The U.S. Senate, led by Estes Kefauver of Tennessee, probes organized crime.

March 29 — Julius and Ethel Rosenberg and Morton Sobell are found guilty of selling U.S. atomic secrets to the Soviet Union. The Rosenbergs are sentenced to death; Sobell receives a thirty-year sentence.

April 11 — General Douglas MacArthur is removed as commander of U.S. troops in Korea for unauthorized statements about U.S. foreign policy.

July — Korea cease-fire talks begin and will last for two years.

September 1 — The U.S., Australia, and New Zealand sign a mutual security agreement.

September 4 — Transcontinental television begins with a speech by President Truman in San Francisco.

Fall — J. D. Salinger publishes *Catcher in the Rye.*

1952

April 8 — The federal government seizes the nation's steel mills to prevent a strike. The U.S. Supreme Court rules in June that such a seizure is illegal.

May 26 — France, Great Britain, West Germany, and the United States sign a peace pact.

June 26-27 — The Immigration and Naturalization Act of 1952 is signed, removing racial and ethnic barriers to becoming a U.S. citizen.

November. 1 — The first hydrogen bomb is exploded by the U.S. at Eniwetok in the Pacific Ocean.

1953

May 8 — President Eisenhower reveals that the U.S. has given France $60 million to help fight the Indochina War. Three-fourths of the war's costs will be met by the U.S.

June 19 — Julius and Ethel Rosenberg are electrocuted for their part in World War II espionage.

July 27 — Fighting ends as a result of negotiations in Korea.

1954

January 21 — The first atomic-powered submarine, *Nautilus*, is launched at Groton, Connecticut.

March 1 — Puerto Rican supporters of independence spray the House of Representatives with gunfire, wounding five people.

April 22 — U.S. Senator Joseph McCarthy begins televised hearings into alleged Communists in the army.

May 17 — Racial segregation is ruled unconstitutional in public schools by the U.S. Supreme Court. Voting unanimously, the court finds segregation to be a violation of the 14th Amendment, which guarantees equal protection under the law. The case is known as *Brown vs. the Board of Education of Topeka, Kansas.*

September 8 — The U.S. joins Australia, France, Great Britain, New Zealand, Pakistan, the Philippines, and Thailand in a defense pact known as SEATO — the Southeast Asia Treaty Organization.

December 2 — The Senate votes 67-22 to censure Senator Joseph McCarthy for his behavior during the army investigation hearings.

1955

February 12 — The U.S. agrees to help train the army of South Vietnam.

May 31 — The U.S. Supreme Court orders public schools integrated with "all deliberate speed."

December 1 — Rosa Parks refuses to give up her seat to a white man on a Montgomery, Alabama, municipal bus. Her arrest starts a boycott that results in segregation being declared unconstitutional.

December 5 — The merger of the American Federation of Labor and the Congress of Industrial Organizations makes the new AFL-CIO an organization with fifteen million members.

1956

March 12 — More than one hundred U.S. Congressmen call for resistance to Supreme Court decisions concerning desegregation.

June 29 — The federal Highway Act is signed, marking the beginning of work on the interstate highway system.

1957

April 29 — Voting rights for blacks are confirmed with Congressional passage of a civil rights bill.

September 4 — National Guardsmen bar nine black children who attempt to enroll in Central High School in Little Rock, Arkansas. Federal troops are sent by President Eisenhower on September 24 to enforce desegregation.

Fall ––Jack Kerouac publishes the Beat novel, *On the Road.*

1958

January 31 — *Explorer I*, the first U.S. satellite, successfully orbits the earth.

July-October — Five thousand U.S. Marines are sent to Lebanon to protect the elected government there from being overthrown.

December 10 — The first domestic jet-airline passenger service is begun by National Airlines between New York City and Miami.

1959

January 3 — Alaska becomes the forty-ninth state.

July 21 — The world's first atomic-powered merchant ship, *Savannah*, is launched at Camden, New Jersey.

August 21 — Hawaii becomes the fiftieth state.

September 15-27 — Soviet Premier Nikita Khrushchev makes a transcontinental tour of the U.S., though he is not permitted to go to Disneyland for security reasons.

FURTHER READING

Allen, Robert. *Black Awakening in Capitalist America*. Garden City: Doubleday, 1969.

Broderick, Francis and August Meier. *Black Protest Thought in the Twentieth Century*. Indianapolis: Bobbs-Merrill, 1971.

Davis, Kenneth C. *Don't Know Much About History*. New York: Avon Books, 1990.

Freeland, Richard M. *The Truman Doctrine and the Origins of McCarthyism*. New York: Knopf, 1971.

Griffith, Robert W. *The Politics of Fear: Joseph McCarthy and the Senate*. Rochelle Park: Hayden, 1971.

Hamby, Alonzo L. *Beyond the New Deal: Harry S Truman and American Liberalism*. New York: Columbia University Press, 1953.

Hoffman, Mark S., editor. *The World Almanac and Book of Facts 1994*. New York: World Almanac, 1993.

Kaledrin, Eugenia. *Mothers and More: American Women in the 1950s*. Boston: Twayne Publishers, 1980.

Krohn, Katherine E. *Elvis Presley*. Minneapolis: Lerner Publishing Co., 1994.

Miller, Douglas, and Marion Nowak. *The Fifties: The Way We Really Were*. New York: Doubleday, 1977.

Nichols, Janet. *Women Music Makers*. New York: Walker and Co., 1992.

Oakley, J. Ronald. *God's Country: America in the Fifties*. New York: Dembner Books, 1986.

Parks, Rosa. *My Story*. New York: Dial Books.

Perlman, Marc. *Movie Classics*. Minneapolis: Lerner Publishing Co., 1993.

Sandak, Cass R. *The Eisenhowers*. New York: Crestwood House, 1993.

Stone, I.F. *The Hidden History of the Korean War*. New York: Monthly Review Press, 1969.

Weidhorn, Manfred. *Jackie Robinson*. New York: Atheneum, 1993.

Zinn, Howard. *A People's History of the United States*. New York: Harper Perennial, 1990.

Zinn, Howard. *Postwar America: 1945-1971*. Indianapolis: Bobbs-Merrill, 1973

INDEX

Page numbers in *italic* indicate picture; page numbers in **bold** indicate biography

ACKNOWLEDGEMENTS

The author and publishers wish to thank the following for permission to reproduce copyright material:

Aquarius Library: 815, 817; Bettmann: 821; The Bettmann Archive: 726, 739, 743, 747, 748, 752, 754, 762 (upper), 766, 767, 779, 782, 789, 811, 814, 818, 819, 823, 826, 831, 835, 838, 855; Gems/Redferns: 841; Peter Newark's American Pictures 732, 736, 740, 741, 744, 758, 760, 813, 844; Peter Newark's Historical Pictures: 731, 837; Peter Newark's Military Pictures: *frontispiece*, 735; Popperfoto: 840; Redferns: 843; Brian Shuel/Redferns: 845; Springer/Bettmann Film Archive: 751, 768, 780, 829; UPI/Bettmann: 727, 728, 729, 737, 742, 746, 749, 750, 753, 755, 756, 761, 762 (lower), 764, 765, 770, 771, 773, 774, 777, 781, 784, 786, 787, 790, 791, 792, 796, 797, 798, 799, 801, 802, 803, 804, 805, 806, 816, 827, 833, 836, 842, 848, 849, 850, 851, 852, 853 (both), 854, 856; UPI/Bettmann N.Y. Journal American Photo from International: 800; UPI/Bettmann Newsphotos: 759, 776, 794, 808, 810, 820, 825, 834, 857.

The illustrations on pages 775, 785, 788, and 807 are by Rafi Mohammed.

Page numbers in *italic* indicate picture; page numbers in **bold** indicate biography